POLICY PAPERS

NUMBER 40

SYRIA BEYOND THE PEACE PROCESS

DANIEL PIPES

THE WASHINGTON INSTITUTE FOR NEAR EAST POLICY
WASHINGTON, D.C.

Library of Congress Cataloging-in-Publication Data

Pipes, Daniel, 1949-
    Syria beyond the peace process/Daniel Pipes.
    p.cm.—(Policy papers/The Washington Institute for Near East Policy;
no. 40)
    Includes bibliographical references.
    ISBN 0-944029-64-7

    1. Syria—Politics and government. I. Title. II. Series.
DS98.2.P56 1995
320.95691—dc20   95-39452
                                                                        CIP

THE AUTHOR

Daniel Pipes, editor of the *Middle East Quarterly* and adjunct scholar of The Washington Institute for Near East Policy, wrote this study as a visiting fellow at The Washington Institute. A historian, Dr. Pipes has written two previous books on Syria: *Greater Syria: The History of an Ambition* (Oxford University Press, 1990) and *Damascus Courts the West: Syrian Politics, 1989-91* (Washington Institute for Near East Policy, 1991).

Dr. Pipes dedicates this study to those many who have paid for what Amos 1:3 terms "crime after crime of Damascus."

CONTENTS

ACKNOWLEDGMENTS

The author benefited from conversations with Deborah E. Bodlander, Patrick Clawson, Raymond Cohen, Paul Jureidini, Hilal Khashan, George Nader, Danielle Pletka, Walid Phares, and the participants at a Washington Institute workshop in July 1994. He also learned from several individuals who asked not to be publicly acknowledged.

Dr. Pipes thanks Nick Beckwith, Carmel David, and Louis E. Nosce for help with research. References to radio and television broadcasts derive from transcripts made by the Foreign Broadcast Information Service *Daily Report*, as do many items from Middle Eastern newspapers. Some translations have been slightly amended for consistency of style.

To keep down the length of this study, Dr. Pipes has treated only lightly those subjects covered in previous Washington Institute studies on Syria (Patrick Clawson on the economy; Michael Eisenstadt on the military; Ze'ev Schiff on relations with Israel; *Supporting Peace*, a study assessing a prospective deployment of U.S. troops on the Golan Heights; and the author's own study on Syrian politics in the years 1989-91).

PREFACE

For more than two decades, U.S. efforts to broker peace between Israel and its Arab neighbors have included an important corollary: making peace with Israel and earning the support of the United States implies a turn to the West and acceptance of certain Western values, attitudes, and policies. As a result, Egypt jettisoned its Soviet alliance; the PLO renounced terrorism and has submitted to a popular election; and Jordan abandoned its close links to the rogue regime in Baghdad. None of these peace partners has become a full, open democracy, but the improvements have been structural and fundamental.

Syria, however, has held out, refusing to budge far from its brutality at home and support for terrorism abroad, even as it seeks U.S. assistance in engineering a peace with Israel. Nevertheless, because the prospect of Israel-Syria peace is so important to U.S. regional interests, Washington has submerged much of its outrage at ongoing Syrian practices so as to pursue an elusive Israel-Syria diplomatic breakthrough. Though a wide range of sanctions remain in place against Syria, these have been tempered by an equally wide range of official contacts at the highest levels, which almost surely sends mixed messages to Syria about U.S. interests and priorities.

In this Policy Paper, his second Washington Institute monograph, noted Middle East expert Dr. Daniel Pipes offers an alternative approach to dealing with the regime of Hafez al-Assad. Analytically, he argues for viewing Syria through a wider lens than just the Arab-Israeli peace process. Operationally, he calls for a new mix of policies, which takes advantage of Syrian weakness to press for basic changes in Syrian behavior on issues critical to U.S. interests. With more vinegar and less honey, he contends, the United States has the potential to achieve what it seeks in the peace process—a full and warm Israel-Syria peace—as well as to get Syria to commit to join the West in an alliance against what he views as the region's most dangerous challenge: radical fundamentalism.

Today, four years after the Madrid peace process, progress in Israel-Syria talks is still measured in winks and nods, as opposed to the treaties and agreements reached on the Jordanian and Palestinian tracks. In challenging the conventional wisdom on Syria, this Policy Paper offers a fresh, provocative approach to tackling the Assad conundrum. We hope it will serve as a useful contribution to the policy debate.

Michael Stein   Barbi Weinberg
President   Chairman

January 1996

EXECUTIVE SUMMARY

Conventional political analysis of the Syrian regime of Hafez al-Assad focuses too heavily on the narrow questions relating to the Arab-Israeli peace process and too lightly on Assad's own interests, political ambitions, and style of decisionmaking. Analytically, such tunnel vision misrepresents Assad's priorities, in which regime survival, continuity of Alawi supremacy, and suzerainty over Lebanon are ranked above the reclamation of the Golan Heights. Operationally, this approach limits Washington's ability to secure other regional interests (e.g., fighting terrorism, preventing the proliferation of weapons of mass destruction, promoting human rights, and combating the spread of radical Islamic fundamentalism) and, ironically, reduces U.S. leverage to win peace process concessions from Damascus.

While the pursuit of Arab-Israeli peace justly remains the dominant U.S. interest in the Levant, it is important to assess Syrian politics through a wider political lens. Since coming to power in 1970, Assad has imposed a brutal, authoritarian police state that has brought an unprecedented measure of stability to historically anarchic Syria and *inter alia* elevated his long-persecuted Alawi minority to control of the regime's political and military apparatus. From the start, regime maintenance and ensuring a family succession have been Assad's top priorities, with all other policies—from the Arab-Israeli conflict to inter-Arab relations to support for international terrorism—instrumental tools in the effort to keep stability and security at home.

Assad's alliance with the Soviet Union was a critical element in this effort and the collapse of communism was a shock to Assad and the Syrian elite. Responding to that shock—and thereby finding a new way to secure the longevity of Alawi rule—has dominated Syrian politics since 1989. By definition, this search for a new safeguard of regime security has required Assad to be pragmatic, not ideological, on issues ranging from the confrontation with Israel to his commitment to socialism.

On none of these issues, however, could Assad bring himself to make a complete conversion because it might threaten regime stability. Domestically, economic reform has gone little beyond loosening restrictions for importers and foreign investors, with the government bureaucracy still controlling much of the economy; attempts at political liberalization have been transparent and superficial. On the peace process, Assad dropped technical obstacles to negotiations with Israel years ago and concessions by Israel have left the substantive gaps between Syrian and Israeli positions remarkably slim, yet there remains little prospect of Assad actually making peace with the Zionists unless wholly on his terms. Through it all, Assad has sought to establish a new relationship with the United States, not to replace the Soviet umbrella but to provide insurance against Syria's two main foes—pro-West Turkey and pro-West Israel—at a time of profound military weakness and vulnerability. Yet even here, Assad balances his effort to build ties with Washington, exemplified by Syria's participation in the anti-Iraq Gulf War alliance, to his dogged commitment to maintain other alliances with the world's few remaining "rogue states," such as Iran and North Korea.

Syrian-Turkish tension is perhaps the most overlooked potential flashpoint in the world. The two countries differ over a wide range of issues: territory (Syria claims the Turkish province of Hatay); water resources (Syria fears Turkish manipulation of Tigris and Euphrates water); and most importantly, terrorism (Syria actively supports the Kurdish Workers Party, PKK). So far, only Turkish forbearance has prevented a hot conflict between these two countries.

Given Syria's location between two key allies—Turkey and Israel —the United States has a strong interest in containing Syrian mischief-making and in promoting peace and stability in the Levant. Despite Syria's history of rogue behavior, including indirect participation in the bombing of Pan Am airlines Flight #103, Washington's approach to Damascus has always been tinged with as much sorrow as anger. While stiff sanctions have been imposed on Syria for its participation in terrorism and the international narcotics trade, the prospect of wooing Assad into peace with Israel has tempered U.S. policy, leading to four presidential summits with Assad (one each with Carter and Bush, and two by Clinton) and dozens of visits to Damascus by U.S. secretaries of state, both Republican and Democratic.

This nuanced policy has registered some successes but at a time of U.S. strength and Syrian weakness, much more can be achieved. The objective of U.S. policy should not be to undermine Assad but to take advantage of his weakness to force an evolution in his policies that advance U.S. interests in peace and security and that build upon the common U.S.-Syrian interest in combating radical Islamic fundamentalism. In return for the cooperation and support he seeks as a way to protect Alawi rule, Washington should demand a warm peace with Israel, a withdrawal from Lebanon, and an end to support for the PKK insurgency against Turkey. This will force Assad to choose between Iran and America, between terrorism and stability, between proxy conflict and peace. If pursued creatively and vigorously—through shifts in declaratory, diplomatic, regulatory, and potentially even military policy—this approach can work because it offers Assad U.S. support for what he seeks most: regime survival.

I ASSAD'S POST-SOVIET PREDICAMENT

Peace in the Middle East can't be achieved [only] through a reconciliation between Israel and the Palestinians.

—President Süleyman Demirel of Turkey[1]

In the Prism of the Peace Process

In the course of an informative October 1993 interview on the *MacNeil/Lehrer NewsHour*, Charlayne Hunter-Gault quizzed President Hafez al-Assad about current issues. What did he think of the just-signed Declaration of Principles between Israel and the Palestine Liberation Organization (PLO)? Did he feel "the earth tremble" when Yitzhak Rabin and Yasser Arafat shook hands? Was he ready to compromise with Israel about the Golan Heights? How far apart was his position from Israel's? Every one of Hunter-Gault's thirty-one questions to Assad, in fact, pertained to Syrian negotiations with Israel, the peace process.[2]

Hunter-Gault does not stand alone in her emphasis. Nearly all American discussion of Syria focuses on that country's relations with Israel. In a typical statement after meeting with Assad, Secretary of State Warren Christopher said he and the president had covered "a wide range of topics, but the great majority of the time was spent discussing progress in the [Syrian-Israeli] peace negotiations."[3] Every question asked of Presidents Clinton and Assad after their two

---

[1] *Hürriyet*, October 12, 1993.

[2] *MacNeil/Lehrer* used only a small portion of the interview in its October 1, 1993 broadcast but Syrian Arab Television broadcast the entire interview one day later. For excerpts from the latter transcript, see "Asad on the Israel-PLO Accord," *Middle East Quarterly* (March 1994): 81-85.

[3] August 4, 1993. Judith Wrubel, ed., *Peacewatch: The Arab-Israeli Peace Process and U.S. Policy* (Washington, DC: The Washington Institute for Near East Policy, 1994), 65. So much American attention to this issue causes U.S. allies to follow suit; thus, President Hosni Mubarak of Egypt reported that his talks in Damascus during July 1994 dealt "mainly" with the peace process (Middle East News Agency, July 24, 1994).

meetings in 1994 pertained to the peace process. Every mention of Syria in a major May 1994 policy address by Anthony Lake, Clinton's national security advisor, concerned the peace process. Recent American books on Syrian politics bear such titles as *Syria and the Middle East Peace Process* and *The Superpowers and the Syrian-Israeli Conflict.*[1]

Looking at Syria through the prism of its relations with Israel reflects two facets of American foreign policy: a widespread media and scholarly fascination with Israel and a governmental emphasis on ending the Arab-Israeli conflict.

But Syria is a country of some fourteen million persons; seeing it only as an adjunct of Israel ignores other aspects of that country, including much that directly concerns Americans.[2] On the positive side, for example, Damascus stands as a Middle Eastern stalwart resisting the surge of fundamentalist Islam; and Syria's oil industry, producing over 600,000 barrels per day, has recently emerged as a significant exporter. On the negative side, Assad's record of repression in Syria deeply offends American sensibilities. Damascus's occupation and domination of Lebanon harms American interests and runs counter to U.S. principles. Its support for terrorist organizations has made it complicit in the death of more American citizens than any other state in the past two decades. Over a quarter of the heroin entering the United States comes from territories under Assad's control. Damascus plays an integral role in a shrinking but still potent network of anti-American regimes extending from North Korea to Iran to Libya. Its support for the Worker's Party of Kurdistan (Partiya Karkerana Kurdistan, or PKK) erodes the stability of Turkey, a NATO ally.

Focusing almost exclusively on the potential for a peace agreement between Israel and Syria slights the full range of important items on the U.S.-Syrian bilateral agenda, thereby skewing the policy debate and permitting a number of false expectations to develop. For example, although there is no necessary connection between the peace process and Syrian support for terrorism (e.g., Syrian support for the anti-Turkish PKK), Syria's officials are confident that if their government reaches an agreement with Israel, the U.S. government will remove it from the list of states sponsoring terrorism; it is not clear that American officials have done much to disabuse Assad of this notion. Similarly, emphasis on the Israel-Syria peace talks makes comment on other items—like Syrian domination of Lebanon—undiplomatic and

---

[1] Alasdair Drysdale and Raymond A. Hinnebusch, *Syria and the Middle East Peace Process* (New York: Council on Foreign Relations, 1991); Helena Cobban, *The Superpowers and the Syrian-Israeli Conflict* (New York: Praeger, 1991).

[2] In this regard, Syria resembles other Arab actors. Americans took interest in Egypt and Lebanon only so long as these countries were closely engaged with Israel in issues of war and peace.

out-of-bounds. Thus, the U.S. government has refrained from even verbally protesting Assad's conquest of Lebanon, fearing that to do so would obstruct Israeli-Syrian negotiations.

Peace process exclusivity also leads to all of Syrian public life being seen through the prism of foreign relations, rather than the other way around. Analysts assess symptoms, not causes. When the *New Republic* argues in an editorial that "Peace with Israel would require a deep change in the nature of [Assad's] regime,"[1] it's got things exactly backwards: changes in the regime must precede peace with Israel. The Golan issue surely has less importance for Assad than, for example, Syria's standing among the Arab states. Rather than concentrate on symptoms—Assad's willingness to allow an Israeli embassy in Damascus or the purposes of his military buildup—we should examine Assad's views of the world and Syria's place in it. Analysts need to focus less on questions like "On what terms will Assad make peace with Israel?" or even "Does Assad intend to make peace with Israel?" but rather on "How will Assad cope with the unpleasant realities of the post-Soviet period?"

This wider perspective turns up several important conclusions:

• While Assad shares with other authoritarian leaders the goal of personal and regime survival, he stands apart from most of them in his willingness to resort to extreme means to achieve his ends. To keep himself and his fellow Alawis in power, he could do anything from destroy a Syrian city (as he did to Hama in 1982) to reverse a lifetime of anti-Zionism and sign a peace treaty with Israel.

• However, Assad has not so far made a choice for peace with Israel (except a peace solely on his terms) and is likely to avoid any compromise unless essential to ensure the stability of his rule. U.S. importuning has little impact on his actions; to affect Assad's actions means altering the calculus of his decisionmaking.

• Assad has successfully developed a relationship with Washington based almost solely on the peace process while preserving a strategic relationship with the Islamic Republic of Iran which violently opposes the same process. This fits into his consistent effort to avoid committing to a policy; in contrast to the bold risk-taking of Anwar al-Sadat, Assad prefers to move two contrary ways at once, thereby retaining options, escape routes, and future possibilities.

• While the West has historically focused on the threat of conflict along the Israel-Syria border, Damascus's most volatile and dangerous relationship today is with Turkey. Terrorism, irredentism, and clashes over water resources make this a potentially hot frontier.

• Despite serious conflicts between Washington and Damascus on a wide range of issues (e.g., terrorism, human rights, narcotics, weapons of mass destruction), the U.S. government should view the possibility

---

[1] *New Republic,* "Courting Damascus," July 14, 1994.

of building bilateral relations through the lens of Assad's potential utility in combating fundamentalist Islam.

• The opportunity exists, therefore, for Washington and Damascus to cooperate as partners in the confrontation with radical Islam. Creating such a partnership, however, requires a fundamental shift in behavior by the Syrian regime.

• To achieve such improvements in Syrian behavior, Washington needs to focus less on the Syrian component of the Arab-Israeli peace process and more on a wide range of bilateral concerns. The nature of the Syrian regime suggests that a policy that relies more on sticks than on carrots is likely to achieve better results.

As these conclusions imply, Hafez al-Assad is the key to Syrian politics. The next chapter reviews his tenure as ruler of Syria since November 1970 and the problems he faces as a result of the collapse of the Soviet Union. The subsequent two chapters look at Assad's place in the context of Syrian communal relations and his recent record in domestic affairs. The final four chapters review his foreign policy, with special attention to Turkey, Israel, and the United States.

The Strongest Weak State

Syria had experienced enormous instability during the quarter-century between independence in 1946 and Assad's coming to power. Not a single ruler in that period had managed to control Syria's fractious and unstable population. Its politics were so volatile, one global analysis of the stability of political leaders during the period 1945–61 finds Syria tied at the very bottom of all eighty-seven states studied.[1] The most successful of those early rulers, Shukri al-Quwwatli, captured the era's political effervescence: "Fifty percent of the Syrians consider themselves national leaders, 25 percent think they are prophets, and 10 percent imagine they are gods."[2] Syria suffered from a weak international position and was the perpetual victim of predatory efforts of control from Baghdad and Cairo. The leadership lurched unpredictably from decision to decision. In 1958, for example, it took the unprecedented step of voluntarily giving up sovereignty and having the country effectively annexed to Egypt.

Assad's immediate Ba'thist predecessors espoused a form of infantile leftism almost totally unrelated to the country's actual needs, making the situation yet more unstable. As made evident by their disastrous performance in 1967 against Israel, Syrian soldiers knew altogether too much about overthrowing leaders in Damascus and too little about fighting on a battlefield.

---

[1]   Bruce M. Russett, et al., *World Handbook of Political and Social Indicators* (New Haven: Yale University Press, 1964), 103–04.

[2]   Malcolm H. Kerr, *The Arab Cold War: Gamal Abdul Nasser and His Rivals, 1958-70* (London: Oxford University Press, 1971), 21.

Hafez al-Assad, who was defense minister at the time, took over in 1970. He overthrew a fellow Ba'thist and quickly consolidated power, imposed order, and brought Syria's turmoil to an end. Even enemies acknowledge that he found "welcome and support" among a population tired of anarchy.[1] Although, as Assad also acknowledges, "all Syrians are known to be politicians,"[2] he eliminated politics from daily life by instituting in Syria what Arab critics have dubbed the *mukhabarat* (intelligence services) state. No fewer than fifteen separate security agencies report to Assad personally, each with separate but overlapping jurisdictions.[3]

Assad dominates Syria's public life to such an extent that the political debate in that country consists of little more than the contending ideas in Assad's head. His prejudices determine policy. The national interest is his interest. While other individuals, groups, and institutions have a say, Assad alone in the end makes the decisions of state. As Moshe Arens, Israel's former minister of defense, has observed, "When talking about Syria, we should remember we are not talking about a country but about a ruler."[4]

Assad also enhanced Syria's place in the world. As a Syrian explains about his country, "It was a homeland influenced by others but became a homeland influencing others."[5] The Egyptian and Iraqi struggle to control Syria came to an end, replaced by an active and powerful Syria which, more than any other state, charted the Levant's course of history. Syria under Assad became the powerbroker in Lebanon and, by virtue of his sponsoring terrorist opposition groups all over the region, a major factor in the political life of Jordan and Turkey. Assad effectively abandoned pan-Arab nationalism in the early 1970s, looking instead to dominate a much smaller area in the Levant; with this, he changed the region's ideological climate. By bringing stability to Syria and pursuing an ambitious foreign policy, he built Syria into what Alasdair Drysdale calls the Middle East's "strongest weak state."[6] Indeed, Vice President 'Abd al-Halim Khaddam has declared, with some justification, that "Syria is the most stable country in the Third World."[7]

---

[1] Mahmud Sadiq, *Hiwar Hawl Suriya* (London: Dar 'Ukaz, 1993), 37.

[2] Syrian Arab Republic Radio, March 12, 1992.

[3] According to Middle East Watch, *Syria Unmasked: The Suppression of Human Rights by the Assad Regime* (New Haven: Yale University Press, 1991), 40; Sadiq, *Hiwar Hawl Suriya,* 128, counts only ten.

[4] Israel Television, May 22, 1991.

[5] *Al-Muharrir,* July 31, 1995.

[6] Alasdair Drysdale, "Syria since 1988: From Crisis to Opportunity," in Robert O. Freedman, ed., *The Middle East After Iraq's Invasion of Kuwait* (Gainesville, FL: University Press of Florida, 1993), 276.

[7] Syrian Arab Republic Radio, April 27, 1993.

Nowhere, however, was Assad's power so evident as in the Arab-Israeli conflict. As ruler of Egypt, Anwar al-Sadat could ignore Syria when he made peace with Israel, but virtually every initiative to resolve the Arab-Israeli relationship in the 1980s foundered when it came up against Assad's objections. Secretary of State George Shultz's fine accord between Lebanon and Israel in May 1983 came to nothing due to Assad's resolve to undo the deal. In 1985-86 King Hussein of Jordan appeared willing to end the conflict with Israel, but Syrian sabotage convinced the king otherwise. The PLO on several occasions in the 1980s flirted with the idea of reaching an agreement with Israel; these too never panned out, in large part because of Syrian influence over the Palestinian movement. Only when Assad came to the bargaining table in 1991 could the Palestinians and Jordanians begin serious negotiations with Israel.

"We Regret the Soviet Collapse More than the Russians Do"
Close relations with the Soviet Union were a key element through most of Assad's rule. Syrian alignment with the Soviet Union began about the time of the very first purchase of Soviet-bloc arms in 1954; the two states became ideologically close when the Ba'th Party took power in March 1963. Assad experienced some tensions with Moscow in his first years but relations blossomed after 1977. While the two states never enjoyed a perfect harmony of interests, their bonds far surpassed the "marriage of convenience" portrayed by some analysts. The Soviet connection had enormous importance, touching many aspects of domestic life and making Damascus part of an international alliance.

In domestic politics, Damascus emulated the Soviet system and adopted many Soviet-type ideological and political characteristics. It controlled speech, persecuted religion, engaged in torture, and made a general mockery of its own laws. The economy came under bureaucratic jurisdiction, with private farms giving way to state-controlled cooperatives and the state taking over what it generously deemed to be "strategic industries."

In public life, too, Syria came to resemble the Soviet Union. Regime slogans about socialism, pan-Arab unity, and anti-Zionism were endlessly repeated by teachers, school books, radio and television shows, movies, youth leagues, museum exhibitions, military manuals, and virtually every other public source of information. As in the Soviet Union, the whole of society was militarized: sixth-graders wore army fatigues in class and learned how to dismantle automatic weapons. Assad developed a cult of personality that in some ways recalled the Stalinist period. Assad and others in the Syrian leadership—especially 'Abd al-Halim Khaddam and Foreign Minister Faruq al-Sharaa—even adopted a Soviet style of speech, beginning with high principles and working back to practical applications.

On the international level, Syria had its assigned part to play in the "socialist division of labor" that arrayed the Soviet bloc in a worldwide effort against the United States and its allies. The Soviets counted on Assad to adhere to their line, and he invariably did on the major issues (although the two differed on what Moscow considered lesser matters, such as Lebanon). Assad was one of the very few leaders, for example, who voluntarily endorsed the Soviet aggression in Afghanistan in 1979-89. Indeed, precisely because he joined the Soviet camp of his own volition and not as a satellite, Assad had special importance to Moscow. The Syrian military became partially integrated into the Soviet system, especially with regard to its navy, air force, and short-range ballistic missiles. So dense and close were Soviet-Syrian military ties, the U.S. Department of Defense in 1985 termed Syria "the centerpiece of Soviet Middle East policy."[1]

In return, the Syrian leadership gained much from the Soviet Union, including weapons, military training, intelligence, financial aid, political support, and diplomatic cover. The Soviets offered themselves as a trading partner willing to take second-rate goods and as a source of safe cultural products. In addition—something often neglected—the leadership in Damascus gained psychological security by participating in a global network. Soviet bloc rulers forwarded Assad's position at international fora, regularly traveled to Damascus, and hosted him in their capitals. The rulers praised each other, exchanged gifts,[2] attended each other's funerals, touted one another's achievements, and trumpeted in the media what the other wanted said about himself. The men of Damascus associated themselves with a large and flourishing alliance, adding much to their self-confidence.

A new era began for Assad in April 1987, when Mikhail Gorbachev publicly signaled his intention to reduce Soviet support. He told Assad that the absence of relations between the USSR and Israel "cannot be considered normal"; worse, he publicly admonished Assad that "the reliance on military force in settling the Arab-Israeli conflict has completely lost its credibility."[3] To make matters more dire yet, the Soviet bloc began to fall in 1989 and was gone by the end of 1991.

This development profoundly affected all aspects of Syrian politics. It established the failure of the Soviet model and turned the psychological benefit of belonging to a powerful international alliance into the liability of association with a losing team. It cut off Syria's advantageous trade relations with the Soviet bloc. It dealt a nearly mortal blow to Assad's goal of attaining "strategic parity" (*al-tawazun al-*

---

[1] Department of Defense, *Soviet Military Power*, 1985, (Washington, DC: U.S. Government Printing Office, 1985), 124.

[2] The Communist Party's U.S. headquarters on West 23rd Street in New York City boasts gifts from the Ba'th Party of Syria in a display case in its board room.

[3] *Pravda*, April 25, 1987.

istratiji) with Israel—that mix of military, economic, and cultural achievement that would permit Syria to face Israel as an equal either on the battlefield or at the bargaining table.

Assad publicly acknowledged the extent of his problems, remarking sourly in early 1992 and hinting of a conspiracy: "The Arabs lost a great deal, and Israel won a great deal, politically, economically, and militarily, so much so that it would appear that what happened had been planned and implemented for the sake of Israel."[1] A few weeks later, referring to changes around the globe, he noted that "the Arabs are not among the winners so far. The winners are the enemies of the Arabs."[2] Assad could have gone further and stated that perhaps more than any other state in the Middle East, his own suffered from the Soviet collapse. Or, as one of his officials admitted, "We regret the Soviet collapse more than the Russians do."[3]

Emotionally, Assad appears still to cling to the old order. In July 1994, he declared a week's mourning on the death of Kim Il Sung and personally went to the North Korean embassy in Damascus to sign the condolence book. When Vietnam's President Le Duc Anh came visiting in May 1995, the two leaders' public statements suggested how much they cherished each other's company. Le spoke of "valiant and beautiful Syria," referred to "an atmosphere of happiness and delight," and recalled a half-century of partnership "to liberate ourselves from the yoke of old colonialism."[4]

As an able politician, however, Assad neither wallowed in nostalgia nor passively succumbed to dreadful circumstances. Rather, he made changes in both domestic and foreign policies. Toward what end? To understand Assad's goals, we look at the key dynamic of Syrian society, tensions between Sunnis and Alawis.

---

[1]   Syrian Arab Republic Radio, March 12, 1992.

[2]   Ibid., April 1, 1992.

[3]   *Christian Science Monitor,* October 29, 1993.

[4]   Syrian Arab Republic Radio, May 5, 1995.

II   KEEPING THE ALAWIS IN POWER

And you, Alawi sect, beware! . . . This is your last chance to change course.
— Muslim Brethren of Syria[1]

Contrary to the impression Assad fosters, few of the world's almost billion Muslims consider him a fellow believer. Rather, they see him as an Alawi, an adherent of a small, secretive post-Islamic religion restricted almost exclusively to Syria. This fact makes Assad an outsider in his own country, with profound implications for his regime and its goals.

Sunni-Alawi Tensions

Some 90 percent of the world's Muslims are Sunnis (the remainder adhere to the Shi'i or 'Ibadi branches) and they constitute almost 70 percent of the population of the Syrian Arab Republic. Like Anglo-Saxon Protestants in the United States, these are the non-ethnics in a heterogeneous society. Through many changes of regime over the centuries, Sunni Arabs comprised the upper classes of Damascus and Aleppo, they controlled the great commercial enterprises, and they owned much of the land. They also ruled Syria between A.D. 636 and 1917, with only few lapses (one of which was the Crusades). The colonial period hardly diminished their position and they regained control of the government at independence in 1946. Through the coups and anarchy of the next twenty years, they retained control. This long heritage of dominance translates into a Sunni assumption that the privileges of power are theirs.

That assumption came to an end in 1966, when a coup brought the Alawis (also known as Alawites, Nusayris, or Ansaris) to power. Alawis in Syria number today about 1.7 million and constitute some 12 percent of the population. The Alawi religion separated from Shi'i

---

[1] *Al-Nadhir,* January 8, 1982. Quoted in Hans Günter Lobmeyer, "Islamic Ideology and Secular Discourse: The Islamists of Syria," *Orient* Hamburg (September 1991): 407.

Islam nearly a thousand years ago and developed into a secretive faith. Alawis have a theology all of their own and do not live by the sacred law of Islam (the *sharia*). At the same time, they have a history of claiming to be Muslims when doing so proves useful. While Muslims historically knew little about the highly elaborated theology of this religion, they rarely found a warm welcome in the forbidding mountain regions inhabited by Alawis; in return, Sunnis and Shi'a traditionally looked upon Alawis as heretics, reviled their religion, and discriminated harshly against them.

In a radical break from their past weakness, Alawis advanced themselves by enrolling disproportionately in the armed forces, then used that power as a base to take over Syria's key political and military positions in February 1966; and five years later, in February 1971, Assad completed the Alawi takeover when he became the country's president. A rich body of evidence points to Assad's basic identity being defined not by his being an Arabic-speaker, a member of the Ba'th party, or a military man, but by his being an adherent of the Alawi religion. Indeed, Middle Eastern critics have long viewed the regime as an instrument of Alawi power; Anwar al-Sadat of Egypt, for example, held it to be "firstly Alawi, secondly Ba'thi, and thirdly Syrian."[1]

On reaching power, Assad set about to extend the Alawi hold on power by placing his co-religionists in the armed forces, the intelligence services, the party, the government, and the civil bureaucracy. To this day, as the U.S. government notes, Alawis "generally enjoy job preferences in the Government."[2] At the top of this structure sits an extremely stable group of some twenty men, mostly Alawi military officers, who have effectively ruled Syria since 1970. Known as the Group (al-Jama'a), they assist Assad in his efforts by loyally holding down key positions of power. The Group forms the ultimate *nomenklatura* of Syria, the tiny oligarchy for whose benefit the entire country is run.

Assad also bonded the other non-Sunni Muslim elements to himself. Isma'ilis, Druzes, Christians, and even Jews found themselves preferring Assad's secular brutality to the opposition's fundamentalist Muslim equivalent. The Armenian manager of Aleppo's famed Baron's Hotel challenged a visitor "to name a Syrian leader who has been better for this country and its minorities." A Jew echoed his sentiment: "I admire Assad; I support him. If it weren't for him, the Moslem Brothers and the Sunni majority would slit our throats."[3] One Jewish leader spoke of Assad's "special care" for his community and another

---

[1]   Quoted in Derek Hopwood, *Syria 1945-1986: Politics and Society* (London: Unwin Hyman, 1988), 97.

[2]   Department of State, *Country Reports on Human Rights Practices for 1993* (Washington, DC: U.S. Government Printing Office, 1994), 1290.

[3]   *Nation,* January 20, 1992; see also *New York Times Magazine,* January 26, 1992.

announced that "We never had it so good as today."[1] Even taking into account the need to survive in a totalitarian state, these statements probably contain some truth.

In contrast, Sunnis have abundant grievances against Alawi rule, not least of which is the ignominy of taking orders from their social and cultural inferiors. From the start, Sunnis resented government policies: socialism reduced their wealth, Alawi dominance insulted their religion, military powerbrokers destroyed the old system of patronage, and authoritarian control meant the effacing of political expression. They also suspected Alawis of seeking revenge for their traditional maltreatment at the hands of Sunnis. In a typical statement, a Damascene told a foreign reporter that "Alawis are destroying the city because they are trying to erase Sunni history."[2] Sunnis see their government through the lens of ethnicity. For example, one writer describes the Murtada Association founded by Hafez al-Assad's brother Jamil as "an ethnic association intended to mobilize the Alawi masses against the Sunni majority on the basis of ethnic incitement."[3] The passage of time has hardened the Sunni-Alawi divide to the point that it dominates the way Syrians interpret domestic politics, and the way they anticipate Syria after Assad's passing.

Once in power, Alawi rulers devised two distinct strategies to deal with discontent among the majority Sunni population. To the families that long ruled the country and dominated its economy, Assad offered a deal: grow wealthy in business but stay out of politics, which would remain an Alawi preserve. The Sunnis for the most part accepted this arrangement and Syria now has two elites, an old economic-cultural elite, predominantly Sunni, and a new military-political leadership, predominantly Alawi. Still, the Sunnis are buffeted each time the system changes, as Joseph Bahout observes: "Ironically, the old bourgeoisie was not only hit by the nationalizations, but is now again threatened by liberalization measures which expose its weaknesses in an open competition with a new set of powerful economic players."[4]

As for the Sunni masses, the rulers tried to deflect attention to their own religious affiliation by imposing a rigorous socialist order, emphasizing class bonds, and maintaining an elaborate set of props to show that the government represents all parts of the population, offers equal opportunity, and is democratic. In particular, the regime constructed a façade of Sunnis in high positions. Men like 'Abd al-Halim Khaddam, Mustafa Tallas, and Faruq al-Sharaa fill lofty and

---

[1] Yusuf Jajati, *al-Sharq al-Awsat*, October 18, 1994; see also *Jerusalem Report*, November 17, 1994.

[2] *Insight*, August 5, 1991.

[3] Mahmud Sadiq, *Hiwar Hawl Suriya* (London: Dar 'Ukaz, 1993), 77.

[4] Joseph Bahout, "The Syrian Business Community, Its Politics and Prospects," in Eberhard Kienle, ed., *Contemporary Syria: Liberalization Between Cold War and Cold Peace* (New York: St. Martin's Press, 1994), 73.

visible cabinet positions. But the people with line authority, especially in times of crisis, are mostly Alawis and other minorities. All but one of the heads of the security agencies, for example, are Alawis. Also symptomatic, at one point, the head of air force security—a key position, especially given Assad's air force roots—was an Alawi officer with the rank of major. Assad's sons fill mid-ranking military positions but enjoy great honor and potential power.

This sleight-of-hand fools few Syrians. A quasi-Marxist scholar had to acknowledge in 1984 that primeval allegiances in Syria are strong and getting stronger:

> even after two decades of socialism and its consequent impact of social stratification, the regional and religious ties (at least in the realm of politics) are emerging to be more important than class ties. In other words, class solidarity is not as strong as religio-regional solidarity.[1]

As ethnic tensions deepened, non-elite Sunnis moved into the opposition and their activities took on a religious cast. Anti-regime activism began in 1964 with riots in Hama led by the Syrian Muslim Brethren and culminated in that same city in February 1982, when a revolt prompted Assad to devastate the city over a ten-day period, leading to a loss of 10,000 to 30,000 lives—up to 10 percent of the city's population. Opposition did not disappear after the destruction of Hama; rather, the Islamic movement in Syria became more careful and patient. Though no longer an organized movement, it continues to exist in Syria, underground, isolated, rabidly anti-Alawi, and still planning to make a bid for power when Assad dies.

The religious tensions of Syrian political life explain why the Islamic movement in Syria has wide popularity among Sunni Muslims and also why it has experienced a greater loss of life than its counterpart in any other Middle Eastern country. They also account for the Islamic movement's non-fundamentalist cast; in Syria, it is more anti-Alawi than anti-Ba'th, more communal than religious. Muslim Brethren literature, for example, hardly ever brings up the usual fundamentalist concern for applying the *sharia*. Rather, its goals consist of the Sunni public agenda. Hans Günter Lobmeyer concludes that while

> the resistance against the Ba'th regime in Syria has an Islamic label, the conflict has little—if anything—to do with Islam. . . . The Islamists are formulating postulates that are not aimed at the establishment of an Islamic

---

[1] Syed Aziz-al Ahsan, "Economic Policy and Class Structure in Syria: 1958-1980," *International Journal of Middle East Studies* 16 (1984): 321. It bears noting, however, that most academic analysts of Syria emphatically deny the validity of what they deem to be a crude "popular caricature of a government purely by and for all Alawis." See Eberhard Kienle, "Introduction," in Kienle, *Contemporary Syria*, 4.

polity like the Islamic Republic of Syria but rather at the political, economic and social interests of their clientele.[1]

The Islamic movement claims that "The [Assad] regime relies on the [Alawi] sect completely and acts in its name; the sect profits from the regime."[2] At times, it threatens Alawis with dire punishment; this has the unintended effect of compelling Alawis to associate more closely with the regime, and of compelling the regime to make survival its top priority. Sunni hostility weighs heavily on the leadership.

As a small minority, the Alawis fear they cannot rule indefinitely against the wishes of almost 70 percent of the population. Their traditionally low place in Syrian society and the undemocratic manner of their ascent make Alawi power likely to be transient. Once the resentful majority of Sunni Muslims reaches power, it will probably exact a terrible revenge. At any rate, that is the worry Alawis express in private. As one analyst recently observed, "Fears among Alawis that they might be victims of a sectarian bloodbath under a majority Sunni regime are not entirely misplaced and provide them with powerful incentives not to relinquish power."[3] Recent wars in Azerbaijan, Yugoslavia, and Rwanda can only reinforce this foreboding—not only has ethnic carnage become widespread, but the outside world does little to stop it. If massacres come to Syria, Alawis will be on their own. This is what Assad presumably seeks to prevent, and it inspires his two chief goals: to control Syria during his own lifetime, then pass power on to his family and co-religionists.

Implications

The hypothesis that Assad makes the survival of his community his top priority has a number of important consequences. It compels him to be a pragmatist; it creates the need for a cult of personality; and (somewhat paradoxically) it constrains him to build consensus among his aides and with the Syrian populace.

Pragmatic, not ideological. As a leader who seeks to survive, Assad follows interests rather than abstract ideals. He conducts foreign relations less with an eye to achieving external goals than to strengthening his regime's grip on power. As a sophisticated practitioner of *Realpolitik* and *raison d'état*, Assad commands from the head, not the heart. In years past, totalitarian methods and alliance with the Soviets presented, in Assad's estimation, the best mechanism to survive. Assad has propounded pro-Palestinian, anti-Zionist policies

---

[1] Lobmeyer, "Islamic Ideology and Secular Discourse," 415-16.

[2] *Al-Watan al-'Arabi,* October 21, 1988. Quoted in Lobmeyer, "Islamic Ideology and Secular Discourse," 405.

[3] Alasdair Drysdale, "Syria since 1988: From Crisis to Opportunity," in Robert O. Freedman, ed., *The Middle East After Iraq's Invasion of Kuwait* (Gainesville, FL: University Press of Florida, 1993), 293.

in the twin hopes of diverting the country's attention from unpleasant realities at home and making common cause with the majority of the Syrian population (which views Damascus as the center of a Greater Syria encompassing all of the Levant, including Mandatory Palestine). Applying this utilitarian standard to Syrian politics clarifies some otherwise puzzling decisions, including the surprisingly close ties to the Soviet Union and the switching of sides in Lebanon's civil war in 1976.

In short, Assad will do whatever he must to stay in power. If democracy prevents the persecution of Alawis, he will consider it. More plausibly, if keeping himself, his family, and the Alawis in power requires becoming an American ally or starting a war with Turkey, so be it. Should circumstances change and anti-Zionism no longer serve his interests, he would make peace with the Jewish state.

Indeed, following the signing of the Israel-PLO Declaration of Principles in September 1993, Assad tacitly admitted that he was not really concerned with the Palestinian cause. With some pique, he noted that then-Foreign Minister Shimon Peres had said, in effect, "Why are you Arabs boycotting us? You have been saying the Palestine question is the core of the conflict. Here we are now, we have reached an agreement."[1] To this argument, Assad responded with impatience, accusing Peres of insulting his intelligence:

> Of course, we have said, and we still say, that the Palestine question is the core of the conflict. It is the core of the conflict in that it was the starting point of hostility. Hence we called it the core of the conflict, but it is not the conflict. . . . The Israelis know they have fought states. All the wars that were fought between Arabs and Israel were wars with states bordering Palestine. As a result of these wars, the core of the conflict that started in Palestine expanded to mean that every occupied Arab territory has become the core of the conflict.[2]

A month later, Information Minister Muhammad Salman made this point more explicitly. The Syrian aim in negotiations, he said, "is to bring about Israel's withdrawal from Syrian and Lebanese territories, recover Jerusalem, and give the Palestinian people their legitimate rights."[3] The lack of any reference to the West Bank and Gaza underscores Syria's true order of priorities.

These admissions point to Assad's real concerns—not Palestinian rights but regaining territory he personally had a part in losing to Israel when he served as air force chief in 1967; not redeeming Arab pride but his own weakness; not ideology but self-interest.

Cult of personality. In addition to a massive and effective machinery

---

[1] This is Assad's paraphrase, Syrian Arab Television, October 2, 1993. In an interview with IDF Radio on October 3, 1993, Peres nearly repeated the words attributed to him: "Certain Arab leaders said they would recognize Israel if we recognized the PLO. We recognized the PLO, but they did not follow through on their part."

[2] Syrian Arab Television, October 2, 1993.

[3] *Al-Diyar* (Beirut), November 2, 1993.

of repression, Assad also feels a need to overawe the Syrian population through a tool common to dictators, the cult of personality. His portraits adorn government offices, stores, private houses. The typical classroom features over a dozen pictures of the "Leader," a railway station wall carries several dozen. Outdoors, placards appear everywhere from busy urban intersections to quiet rural highways, while heroic pictures of him welcome travelers to Syrian cities. Taxi drivers sport decals with a red heart next to a picture of their president, while trains, trucks, buses, and private cars sport the presidential image. Assad turns up on five-story portraits, five and twenty foot-high statues, flags, and tiny decals; his image appears among the meat cuts on display in butchers' shops and on the walls of public toilets. Festivals, holidays, and election campaigns provide the backdrop to an increased dose of Assad portraits strung across the streets and pasted onto walls. Most interesting, his cult even extends to Israeli-controlled territory: a wall in the main square of Majd al-Shams, a Druze village on the Golan Heights, features two posters of Assad.

Assad's name graces a myriad of institutions and places in Syria. Any event of significance takes place under his patronage. Early on, schools inculcate students with the cult: children learn to clap on hearing the president's name and memorize special songs of adulation to their leader. Indeed, when the teacher enters the classroom, students stand and sing in unison, "Our Eternal Leader, Hafez al-Assad." In even the most formal settings, regime spokesmen refer to their country as "Assad's Syria" (*Suriya Asad*). The children's magazine produced by the Ba'th Party, *al-Tali'i,* not only features Assad on many covers and discusses him on the first page of every issue, but it routinely refers to Assad as the "Father-Leader" (*al-Ab al-Qa'id*). More remarkable yet, the magazine lets mothers into its pages but not fathers: Assad has apparently taken their collective place.[1]

Syrian propaganda sometimes imputes a divine quality to Assad and his family. After the July 1992 death of his mother Na'isa, pictures appeared which showed her with a halo, being bowed to by her son Hafez. In Qardaha, the Assad hometown, a large sculpture shows the late Basil al-Assad ascending to heaven on horseback as Hafez bids him farewell—a clear echo of Muhammad's journey. When Assad walks by in person, ordinary Syrians are expected to bow to him. With apparent seriousness, officials refer to him as the Sanctified One (*al-Muqaddas*). Less seriously, some Syrians joke about their "two Gods"—a pungent bit of humor among rigorously monotheistic Muslims.

---

[1] Allen Douglas and Fedwa Malti-Douglas, *Arabic Comic Strips: Politics of an Emerging Mass Culture* (Bloomington, IN: Indiana University Press, 1994), 115-17.

As in Iraq, foreigners find the ruler's ubiquitous presence a bit preposterous. One American journalist described the cult as follows:

> The experience starts at the Jordan border post, which is impossible to miss because it includes a giant photo of President Assad. This proves to be truth in advertising, because the same Assad photo is everywhere in Syria—on buses, hanging from buildings, in offices (the foreign minister has two), behind hotel reception desks. Other countries have had cults of personality, but most of these have had a kind of disembodied feel (Mao, Lenin). What's eerie about the Assad photo is its ordinariness: He wears a white shirt, coat and tie and just the hint of a sardonic smile. It's as if [American criminal] John Gotti staged a coup and had his photograph mounted everywhere.[1]

The presidential election (technically, not an election, but a "renewal of the oath of allegiance") of December 1991 amounted to a sustained bout of glorifying Assad. The government reportedly spent $80 million to stage mammoth rallies, countless banners, and vast street throngs shouting slogans ("By our souls, by our blood, we pledge our lives to you, Oh Hafez of God"). In one surreal event, a group of Syrian Jews carried placards in Hebrew acclaiming the president ("Yes, forever, to Hafez al-Assad from the Jewish youth of Damascus"); in another, demonstrators carried a sign calling themselves "Political Prisoners for Assad."[2]

Assad hardly needed these exertions to win the election. In the classic Soviet style, voting took place under the watchful eyes of policemen and ballots contained just one name—Assad's. The "ayes" won by a margin of 6,726,843 to 396; just one person in 17,000 voted against the president (and nine-tenths of those were apparently cast at Syrian embassies abroad).[3] Foreigners might deride Assad's rule as "One Man, One Idea, Once," but the official media treated the returns as a wonder of democracy: a government spokesman prefaced his announcement that Assad had won 99.994 percent of the vote with a long discourse on "the establishment of a solid democratic system" in Syria.[4]

Also, the day the results were announced, television news devoted twenty-three of its thirty minutes to Assad standing on a balcony, wordlessly accepting the cheers from his supporters below. When Assad

---

[1] Paul Gigot, "Syria Diary: Assad Has a Deal We Can Refuse," *Wall Street Journal*, December 27, 1993.

[2] *Spectator*, December 7, 1991.

[3] Curiously, Assad's percentage has gone up in each of his four elections, from a mere 99.2 in 1971, to 99.6 in 1978, to 99.9 in 1985. Not everyone understood the results in the approved spirit, as a raft of jokes indicated. In one, it's said that the ballot has two choices, "Yes" and "Inform next-of-kin." In another, an aide reports delightedly to President Assad he won the vote 6,726,843 against 396, yet Assad shows no pleasure at the news. "What more could you want," asks the aide, "when only 396 people voted against you?" "Their names," replies a dour Assad.

[4] Syrian Arab Republic Radio, December 3, 1991.

finally commented on his "electoral" victory in December 1992, he spoke in the tradition of totalitarian kitsch:

> Brothers and sons, beloved ones, sons of this great people: I speak to you today to convey my sincerest love, greatest appreciation, and deepest gratitude. I speak to you, overflowing with feelings. It is an inexhaustible spring of love for each and every one of you; a spring that will never die down, but, rather, will grow with time. No end to it can be seen and I see no limits to it.[1]

Like other absolute rulers, Assad uses rare public appearances to turn himself into a father-figure with divine attributes, high above politics. He might appear on television for a full hour, reviewing a military parade, wordlessly accepting the apparently joyous acclamation of his soldiers. If meetings with the Syrian public have turned into "circuses of hollow adulation,"[2] they are also calculated to glorify Assad's persona and maximize his power. The proliferating pictures, the near-unanimous elections, and the rare public appearances all serve the same ends: to strengthen Assad's rule and help him negotiate crises.

Building consensus. At the same time, as an intelligent ruler from a reviled minority, Assad understands the inherent fragility of his regime. Accordingly, he rules with as light a touch as possible. Unlike Saddam Hussein, he relies on coercion only when necessary and avoids making enemies gratuitously. Indeed, to strengthen his position, Assad routinely brings the Group into his decisionmaking process, takes its views into account, and at times makes the effort of building a consensus among its members.

Assad even appears to take Syrian public opinion into account. For example, the Syrian authorities extract low taxes from the population; according to one member of parliament, taxes provide just 30 percent of government total spending.[3] Unlike failed dictators elsewhere, such as Nicolae Ceausescu of Romania, Assad prefers to go without money than to extract funds from a disaffected population. Patrick Clawson goes so far as to suggest that "When commentators write about Assad's brutality and his iron grip on Syria, they should also contemplate the limits to his rule" as indicated by his policy of light taxation.[4]

Similarly, though the 1982 massacre in Hama remains a powerful lesson for anti-regime Sunnis, Assad and his aides speak of fundamentalist Islam in gentle tones. In one interview, for example,

---

[1] Syrian Arab Republic Radio, December 4, 1992.

[2] *Middle East International,* January 8, 1993.

[3] Elyas Nijma, *Middle East Economic Digest,* May 8, 1992.

[4] Patrick Clawson, *Unaffordable Ambitions: Syria's Military Build-Up and Economic Crisis,* Policy Paper Number Seventeen (Washington, DC: The Washington Institute for Near East Policy, 1989), 30-31.

Assad said that if he "were a younger man and an ordinary citizen who sees what is going on around me in the Arab homeland, then I might find myself within [the fundamentalist] movement because, as an enthusiastic young man, I would judge things hastily."[1]

'Abd al-Halim Khaddam spoke even more mildly. "Regarding Syria," he said, "we have no anxiety about or problem with a fundamentalist Islamic movement, or a fundamentalist Christian movement. . . . In Syria there are several trends. There are Marxist, Pan-Arab, and Islamic trends. . . . We have no problem with any of these trends."[2] Such caution signals perhaps a desire to ease passions.

The Syrian leadership professes not only to take public opinion seriously but even to fear the consequences of disregarding it. As Assad quotes himself in conversation with a Western official, "You always talk to us about Israel's public opinion and make us feel as if we have no public opinion but are a herd of sheep. I think you are way off the mark in this assessment. Our public opinion supports us as long as we support public aspirations and just causes."[3] Sharaa warns Israelis "that a step taken by the Syrian leadership toward peace . . . could be sometimes a negative thing and counterproductive among the Syrian public opinion."[4] Assad himself expresses this thought in a strikingly frank way: "I am confident that I enjoy massive popular confidence in our country, and yet, if I did something the Syrian masses interpreted as being contrary to their aspirations, I might pay the price as others did"[5]—an apparent allusion to Arab leaders (such as King 'Abdullah, Anwar al-Sadat, Bashir Jumayyil) who were assassinated for negotiating peace with Israel. Though perhaps a pretext for adopting tough policies *vis-à-vis* Israel, this caution probably also reflects serious concerns.

At times, of course, Assad acts ruthlessly and imposes his will on the Syrian public. This happened in 1974, when he signed a disengagement agreement with Israel; in 1976, when he backed a Christian coalition in Lebanon against Muslims and Palestinians; in 1980, when he supported Iran in its war with Iraq; in 1982, when he destroyed large portions of Hama to extirpate the Muslim Brethren; and in 1990, when he joined the anti-Iraq coalition. In these cases, however, it appears that Assad thought long and hard before he committed to an unpopular course; in 1990, for example, it took forty days before he defined a policy on Iraq's invasion of Kuwait.

---

[1]   Syrian Arab Television, November 23, 1992.

[2]   Radio Monte Carlo, November 16, 1992.

[3]   Syrian Arab Television, December 1, 1994.

[4]   Israeli Television Channel One, October 7, 1994.

[5]   Syrian Arab Television, October 2, 1993.

III DOMESTIC DEVELOPMENTS

> The Levant generally, and especially Syria and Damascus, is the focus, the hot-bed of jealousy, intrigue, plots, and mischief.
>
> —Isabel Burton[1]

Untoward developments of the past decade forced Hafez al-Assad to make changes in fundamental aspects of his rule. Near-bankruptcy in 1986 meant having to open up the economic system from what had been Soviet-style central control. The Soviet collapse in 1989-91 compelled him to court the West by decreasing repression at home and softening his foreign policy. Assad's poor health compels him to make plans for succession.

Economics

Like many other non-Western countries, Syria went through a cycle in the past five decades of weak-state capitalism followed by strong-state socialism and is now finding its way back to an accommodation between the two. A first major shift took place in 1958, when Syria's government delivered the country over to Egypt's Gamal Abdel Nasser to form the United Arab Republic. Though the UAR came to an end in 1961, state intervention became the rule from then on, peaking in the period 1966-70. On coming to power, Assad somewhat reduced the state's obstructionism even as he increased its role in the economy. These changes, known as the first *infitah* (opening), were carried out in a period of prosperity and from a position of strength. Years of command economy led, however, to a decline in productivity. Short-term infusions of aid—from the Soviet bloc, the oil-exporting states, and Syrian workers abroad[2]—masked the extent of this decline for another decade, but by 1980 it could no longer be hidden.

---

[1] Isabel Burton, *The Inner Life of Syria, Palestine, and the Holy Land*, vol. 1 (London: Henry S. King, 1875), 113.

[2] *Financial Times* (July 28, 1995) estimates total aid in the period 1975-95 at $35 billion.

Reforms. Economic stagnation prompted the regime, starting in 1983, to initiate a second "opening." This reform increased the scope of private capital, permitting it to enter previously prohibited areas (such as tourism) and to operate with fewer restrictions (for example, retaining a higher percentage of foreign currency). The authorities hoped to profit from taxes on the private ventures and so save the state companies from bankruptcy. The effort had little success. Half-hearted efforts to cap government spending and reduce imports had meager results; capital continued to dry up and productivity declined. The standard of living plummeted by more than half between 1981 and 1987. By 1991, Syria's foreign debt reached an estimated $16 billion.

Assad embarked on a third, most serious, round of economic reforms soon after the Kuwait War. This "opening" had several main aspects: making Syria a tourist destination, building the oil industry, inviting private investment, and encouraging exports. A four-page advertising spread in the *New York Times* sold the country's charms for visitors this way: "Syria has everything a tourist could want—variety, good climate, spectacular sites, fine food and very hospitable people to whom every stranger may be counted as a friend."[1] The government helps build infrastructure by sponsoring the State Institute for Tourism and a variety of other institutions. It has ambitious plans for tourism, hoping within just a few years to build and fill a seven-fold increase in the number of hotel beds in the country, to one hundred thousand. These efforts met with some success, as the number of tourists in 1993 reached 1.9 million, a 10 percent gain over 1992. Of the visitors, 1.4 million were Arabs and half a million were non-Arabs.

Oil production quadrupled in a decade, from about 150,000 barrels per day in 1985 to over 600,000 barrels per day in 1995. Damascus now exports over $3 billion a year, of which it nets more than $2 billion, funds which provide the motor for an impressive rate of economic growth. At the same time, the country is becoming perilously dependent on oil revenues, which constitute over 70 percent of export earnings. Worse, Syria's oil prospects are not sterling, what with recoverable reserves of less than eight years (at the present rate of production) and foreign oil companies closing shop because they have been overly squeezed by the Syrian authorities.

Perhaps most important of the reforms, Law No. 10 for the Encouragement of Investment, came into effect in May 1991. It fosters investment in Syria by private interests, be they Syrian, expatriate Syrian, Arab, or foreign. The law creates a Higher Council for Investment which issues licenses for new projects, provides exemptions from taxes for up to seven years, permits foreign exchange accounts in

---

[1] *New York Times*, November 17, 1991. The text of this advertisement, written by Michael Frenchman, provides a fairly candid presentation of Syrian circumstances to a presumed skeptical American audience.

Syria's commercial bank, and provides for the repatriation of profits and interest.[1] Four years after its passage, over $5.6 billion had entered Syria under the terms of Law No. 10; and while more than three-quarters of that amount was in hard currency, half of it went for consumption rather than investment, so income has been modest. To the Syrian authorities' disappointment, few Westerners have invested; instead, Syrian and Lebanese expatriates and friendly foreign governments (such as the Chinese) have produced much of the funding.

In part, Westerners have shied away from investing in Syria because the reforms left the old socialist structure substantially standing. A huge public sector dominates the heights of the economy, subsidies and price controls affect most transactions, and stifling foreign exchange controls remain in place. No plans exist to sell off state-owned institutions and a single state-owned commercial bank serves the entire country. While Law No. 10 exempts foreign currency transactions from Law No. 24 of 1986, which set out long prison terms for Syrians caught possessing foreign currency, the older law remains unrepealed and still potentially applicable. (One analyst, Volker Perthes, finds a method in this madness: by keeping the 1986 law on the books, the regime retains the right to prosecute entrepreneurs, and so keeps them vulnerable and weak.)[2]

From a consumer point of view, the high expectations of 1991 have been largely disappointed. While many more foreign goods are available (cars in particular) and travel abroad is more often permitted, not much has changed for most Syrians. *Le Monde* exaggerates only some when it writes that clean, comfortable, and cheap mini-buses are "the only tangible and positive sign of the timid economic opening."[3]

Things look better from a macroeconomic point of view. As a leading party figure put it,

> Last year's economic growth rates registered satisfactory figures and showed steady development in qualitative and quantitative progress. . . in comparison with 1992, the GNP grew at a rate of 17.5 percent in 1993 in current prices. This growth rate becomes 10 percent if it is measured with fixed prices. This is a high and satisfactory rate.[4]

---

[1] *Al-Hayat* (London), May 13, 1991.

[2] Volker Perthes, "The Private Sector, Economic Liberalization, and the Prospects of Democratization: The Case of Syria and Some Other Arab Countries," in Ghassan Salamé, ed., *Democracy without Democrats? The Renewal of Politics in the Muslim World* (London: I.B. Tauris, 1994), 258-59. The old law recalls a Syrian joke circulating in the mid-1980s: "What do you get for the dollar?" "Twenty years."

[3] *Le Monde*, March 3, 1993.

[4] Abdullah al-Ahmar on Syrian Arab Republic Television, March 8, 1994.

Investment has multiplied, privately-owned businesses have doubled, and the growth rate remains an impressive 5 to 8 percent. Oil revenues have made a great difference, as has the retreat of the state from the economy.

Analysis. Why did Assad increasingly open the Syrian economy after 1980? It appears that he realized economic weakness imperiled his rule. A growing economy would strengthen the government against external foes; it would also make the regime's opponents less likely to risk all in challenging the Alawi regime. Finally, as one Syrian put it, as long as Syria has food, "no one can exert pressure on us."[1]

Circumstantial evidence suggests that Assad relied on strictly political criteria to decide which reforms to implement, explaining their haphazard and inconsistent nature. For example, politics limited private firms to certain areas of activity, otherwise they would compete directly with politically loyal elements, and that would not serve Assad's purposes. Substantial vested interests—the ruling elite, the security services, and the large number of public sector employees—benefit from the way things were and so resist change. (The regime directly employs some 450,000 people and indirectly 40 percent of the labor force; they and their dependents constitute a large percentage of the country's population.)

According to Steven Heydemann, the Assad regime is trying to accomplish two almost contradictory goals. It

> must simultaneously persuade the private sector of its sincerity and commitment to reform, without which it would abstain from investing, while persuading its clients and beneficiaries that their position is secure, that they will be protected from the demands of liberalization, and that economic reform will not interrupt their privileges and benefits. This requirement has forced the regime to sacrifice coherence in its economic rhetoric to the preservation of flexibility in its economic policies. . . . These mixed messages, and policies to match, have become a familiar part of the regime's approach to managing economic reform.

For these reasons, "liberalization has not brought about a general renegotiation of the populist coalition that has helped sustain the regime for three decades. It has instead produced a much more limited set of semiprivate bargains, or narrow and exclusive pacts."[2]

The leadership presents stability during the Assad era as something beneficial both to Syrians and to potential investors. Thus, Prime

---

[1] *Al-Hayat* (London), July 11, 1994. David Waldner convincingly shows that economic exigencies were not the reason for Assad's opening toward the West. See "More than Meets the Eye: Economic Influence on Contemporary Syrian Foreign Policy," *Middle East Insight*, (May-June 1995): 34-37.

[2] Steven Heydemann, "Taxation without Representation: Authoritarianisim and Economic Liberalization in Syria," in Ellis Goldberg, et al., eds., *Rules and Rights in the Middle East: Democracy, Law, and Society* (Seattle: University of Washington Press, 1993), 96-97.

Minister Mahmud al-Zu'bi declared that "Syrian Arab society is unique in that it is a secure and stable society enjoying a high sense of nationalism."[1] This outlook appears to convince a number of businessmen, living both inside and outside Syria. Asked about political liberalization, a prominent industrialist replied, "All we want is economic freedom and political stability; for us, democracy often means a coup d'état every two years."[2] When a Syrian newspaper asked a Saudi investor what he found special about Syria, he replied "Stability. We feel more secure in Syria than in any other country."[3]

These high hopes for stability notwithstanding, the Syrian economy appears likely to have a bumpy road ahead. Like many other authoritarian rulers (e.g., the Shah of Iran and China's Deng), Assad seeks to open the market while continuing to impose a strict dictatorship. This implies two problems. First, the economy is unlikely truly to take off so long as the regime's economic policies depend on its political requirements; indeed, the growth rate appears to have nosedived from 1993 to 1994 by some 30-40 percent. Second, to the extent that economic growth does occur, it implies that some people not loyal to the regime acquire an independent power base, possibly emboldening them to engage in anti-regime activities. In the Syrian case, their belonging to the Sunni majority makes the issue yet more ticklish. While it looks like Assad accepts this reality (his government no longer stigmatizes businessmen as it once did, but enjoins them to become partners) the economic reform package appears to be guided by an overriding concern not to give up more control than absolutely necessary. If Assad can in fact retain political control of Syria through the course of economic liberalization, he will have achieved something virtually unprecedented. Interestingly, many analysts believe he can do just this. Thus, Volker Perthes argues that "Economic liberalization, the Syrian case tells us, is possible, and quite successfully so, without being paralleled by substantial political change."[4]

"Sham" Democracy

Assad also made changes in the political realm, but no more than absolutely necessary. With the crumbling of the Soviet model and a goal of improving relations with the United States, he began to ease up slightly on his population in 1989, freeing an initial batch of political

---

[1] *Al-Ba'th* (Damascus), November 19, 1992.

[2] Quoted in Joseph Bahout, "The Syrian Business Community, Its Politics and Prospects," in Eberhard Kienle, ed., *Contemporary Syria: Liberalization between Cold War and Cold Peace* (New York: St. Martin's Press, 1994), 80.

[3] *Tishrin*, August 23, 1994.

[4] Volker Perthes, "Stages of Economic and Political Liberalization," in Kienle, *Contemporary Syria*, 71. Virtually all of Perthes's nine colleagues contributing to this volume agree with him.

prisoners. In 1990, the regime lifted the nearly permanent emergency law provisions, invited some Syrians to return home, permitted mosque preachers to criticize limited aspects of the government's policies, and allowed opposition candidates for the parliamentary elections of May 1990 (and again in August 1994) to speak out on economic issues. It released some 1,500 Palestinians in May 1991 and 4,000 political prisoners during a twelve-month period in 1991-92.

Political restrictions softened in other ways, too. The press aired complaints during 1992 about government agencies disseminating "worthless information," the "ridiculously low" tax on corporations, the People's Assembly not taking up the state budget until six months past schedule, and the unjust restrictions on salaries for state employees.[1] They also began discussing problems hitherto ignored, such as criminal activity in the resort area of Zabadani. Perhaps no issue irritated Syrians as much as the perpetual electricity cuts—typically three hours a day in fashionable urban areas, eighteen hours in rural regions—and a number of these got vented in the media. In addition, commentators expressed their disgust with government offices that "don't give a damn" about the economic havoc of the power shortages.[2] In classic fashion, commentators and letters to the editor could take pot-shots at his cabinet as long as they never criticized Assad himself. (Graffiti artists, however, were not so polite; "Oh Hafez, we gave you our loyalty, now give us some electricity," read a typical example.)

The rulers did permit a slight cultural opening. Film director Muhammad Malas received state support for a critical and introspective film, *Night,* that ostensibly dealt with Syrian politics before Assad's rule but replete with references to current politics. Heavy metal bands play in Damascus—so long as the lyrics are non-political—and the city features some of the Arab world's only cabarets with topless dancers. Fax machines have proliferated, though only on dedicated and licensed lines the government can monitor (and modems remain illegal). The information minister himself acknowledges that there are "tens of thousands" of satellite dishes, not always legally installed, on the roofs of the affluent. Fear seems to be less pervasive:

> People who previously did not want to be seen together in public now meet in cafés and even make the occasional political comment in the presence of a waiter whose accent denotes his origins from the Alawi mountains. No longer do they automatically consider him to be an informer of one of the several police forces.[3]

---

[1] *Al-Ba'th* (Damascus), April 30, 1992; see also *Middle East Economic Digest,* May 8, 1992; *al-Ba'th,* May 11, 1992; and *al-Thawra,* May 31, 1992.

[2] *Al-Ba'th,* quoted in Reuter, September 28, 1993. A Syrian joke has it that a Syrian astronaut radios from orbit to command central that, even though it's night in the Middle East, he can tell exactly where his country is: that's where the lights are blinking on and off.

[3] Eberhard Kienle, "The Return of Politics? Scenarios for Syria's Second *Infitah,*" in

The language of public life changed in small ways, with spokesmen for the regime now making elaborate arguments for the democratic nature of Syrian politics, the pluralism of its economy, and its rigorous rule of law. When a president wins the election with 99.994 percent of the vote, these claims have a slightly ludicrous quality, but the fact that they are made says something about a shift in the regime's sense of popular or international sensibilities and suggests Syria's rulers feel the need to bend a little to the winds of democracy. At the same time, Assad foresees political reforms only in the distant future. Or, as his minister for economy and foreign trade euphemistically phrases it, "When the private sector gains more power and also takes up a greater responsibility in building up the country, the doors will be open for political participation."[1]

In the final analysis, however, the regime's harsh face has stayed essentially in place. The Syrian state still attempts to control the thinking, the speech, and the actions of its citizens. The security services keep an eye on the borders, the media, the schools, and the mosques. Their agents are invariably present wherever Syrians congregate (restaurants, factories, youth clubs, universities, and the like). Jobs which permit the monitoring of movement—including those of taxi drivers, hotel staff, bus stations employees, real estate brokers, travel agents, and even street vendors—are filled by informants who report regularly to the *mukhabarat*.[2]

With some 10,000 political prisoners (or, in Syrian jargon, "persons who have carried out anti-state security acts")[3] out of a population of 14 million, Syria continues to boast one of the highest rates of political incarceration in the world.[4] It is not clear that the releases of political prisoners since 1991 have reduced their numbers, for new ones came in about as fast as the old ones left. Some thousand individuals continue to disappear each year for political reasons. A few political prisoners have been jailed for decades and at least one (Ahmad al-Suwaydani) was put away in 1969, even before Assad had yet taken power.

To make matters worse, Syrian prisons are among the most horrific anywhere.[5] (This is in part the result of advice given by Nazi war

---

Kienle, *Contemporary Syria*, 114.

[1] Muhammad al-'Imadi, *Middle East International*, April 16, 1993.

[2] Middle East Watch, *Human Rights in Syria* (New York: Human Rights Watch, 1990), 43.

[3] Syrian Arab Republic Radio, December 17, 1991.

[4] The Department of State quotes "credible estimates" that put the number between 3,800 and 9,000. The Committee for the Defense of Democratic Freedoms and Human Rights counts 14,000. The May 24, 1991 issue of *al-Hayat* estimates 15,000.

[5] For a detailed, harrowing account of Syrian prisons, see Middle East Watch's *Syria Unmasked: The Suppression of Human Rights by the Assad Regime* (New Haven: Yale University Press, 1991), chapter 5.

criminal Aloïs Brunner who for many years served as a "close security advisor" to Rif'at al-Assad.)[1] Further, in contrast to almost every other government, the Syrian one often holds prisoners in long-term detention without ever charging them with crimes, much less trying them in a courtroom.[2]

The regime's purpose is evidently to break the back of its enemies, an effort that appears to have succeeded. Muslim Brethren and others plot, but no one challenges the regime. As Moshe Ma'oz, an Israeli expert on Syria, comments, "The opposition is in the cemeteries."[3]

Those who work within the system have only marginally more room to maneuver than before. The parliament is permitted to deal with economic issues and problems of everyday life, but not with the affairs of state and certainly not with foreign policy. In this regard, ironically, the role of the People's Assembly in Ba'thist Syria is quite similar to that of the Consultative Council (*Majlis al-Shura*) in reactionary Saudi Arabia.

In the sober language of the U.S. government's human rights report, "Syria is ruled by an authoritarian regime which, although it maintains some of the trappings of democratic government, places virtual absolute authority in the hands of President Hafez al-Asad. . . . [T]here was no basic change in the human rights situation in 1993."[4] In the more dramatic formulation of Freedom House, in terms of freedom, Syria ranks as one of the "twenty-one worst-rated countries" to be found anywhere in the world.[5]

---

[1] Norbert Sakowski, deputy editor-in-chief of *Bunte* magazine, in the *New York Times*, October 28, 1985. Robert Fisk (*Independent*, January 15, 1990) writes that Brunner invented a torture machine in Syria during the 1960s for the extraction of information.

[2] On the treatment of Syrian political prisoners, see two booklets: Amnesty International, *Syria: Long-term Detention and Torture of Political Prisoners* (New York: Amnesty International, 1992); and National Academy of Sciences, *Scientists and Human Rights in Syria* (Washington, DC: National Academy Press, 1993). Despite the horrifying record of the Syrian secret police, some Westerners seem to find them more ridiculous than ominous. David Yallop recounts that "Each [of Syria's many intelligence agencies] appeared to be regularly represented in the foyer of the Sheraton Hotel. The majority [of agents] wore very scruffy suits and sat at all hours in the lounge continuously drinking coffee and appearing to study their newspapers." See *To the Ends of the Earth: The Hunt for the Jackal* (London: Jonathan Cape, 1993), 467.

[3] Moshe Maoz, "Le Carré d'as de Hafez el-Assad," *Politique Internationale* (Spring 1994): 49. Hans Günter Lobmeyer, seeing the opposition's weakness as transient, turns to a different metaphor: "Though it has not yet overcome its crisis and is still far from being able to challenge the regime, it is about to wake up from its slumber." See "*al-Dimuqratiyya hiyya al-hall?* The Syrian Opposition at the End of the Assad Era," in Kienle, *Contemporary Syria*, 88.

[4] Department of State, *Country Reports on Human Rights Practices for 1993* (Washington, DC: U.S. Government Printing Office, 1994), 1284.

[5] Adrian Karatnycky, "Democracies on the Rise, Democracies at Risk," *Freedom Review* (January-February 1995): 6.

Overall, domestic reforms have served as important signs of the potential for change but also of its limits and reversibility. They share three basic features:

• *Utilitarian.* Reforms take place not to improve standards of living or enhance democracy but to ensure the survival of the Alawi regime. Paradoxically, while the reforms are undertaken to sustain the regime, they also slightly diminish its absolute power.

• *Unthreatening.* Despite an enhanced opportunity for Syrians to participate in the political life of their country, they completely lack mechanisms to change their leadership. Just after the fall of Nicolae Ceausescu in 1989, expatriate businessman Omran Adham gained wide attention in the foreign press—and in so doing illustrated the nearly absolute prohibition on dissent within Syria—by writing an open letter to Hafez al-Assad calling for political changes in the country.

• *Reversible.* None of the reforms made thus far indicates basic changes or alterations in course. Rather, Assad has made minor adjustments to adapt to new circumstances while leaving fundamentals largely intact. In many ways, his reforms of the 1990s parallel those initiated by Saddam Hussein in Iraq a decade earlier. In both cases, an authoritarian ruler responded to external pressure by marginally reducing internal controls and re-orienting his foreign policy in favor of the West. Though more than cosmetic, the changes had a specific and temporary purpose. The Iraqi precedent also demonstrates that when circumstances change, the ruler can rapidly undo these improvements and return to his traditional policies.

Though the fall of Ceausescu and other events attending on the Soviet collapse seemed likely to prompt a fundamental reassessment by the Syrian leadership, these developments induced the authorities to make economic and political adjustments at the margins in the hopes that these would prove sufficient. So far, it appears they have.

The Succession Issue

The most important political question in Syria today revolves around the issue of succession. Though posters in a December 1991 referendum on the presidency paid homage to Assad as "Our Eternal Leader," the imminence of succession has fixated regime stalwarts, opponents, and outside observers alike. Assad himself has proudly announced, "I do not have a successor"[1] and is on the record as content to let the Syrian constitution and designated institutions take their course. Few believe this, knowing instead that politics will resume upon Assad's death. How soon that will happen is a matter of intense but furtive speculation, for Assad "clearly regards any discussion or mention of the question of succession as a challenge to his authority."[2]

---

[1] Syrian Arab Television, November 23, 1992.

[2] Itamar Rabinovich, "Stability and Change in Syria," in Robert B. Satloff, ed., *The*

Born on October 6, 1930, Assad is said to suffer from a wide range of physical ills—a weak heart, varicose veins, diabetes, circulatory problems, and leukemia. Most notably, he suffered a heart infarction in November 1983, which laid him low for weeks. Recent photographs show him ill, grayish, and frail. One visitor described Assad as "a bit gaunt but not fatigued," while Ireland's Foreign Minister Dick Spring reported, "You can see in his face that he's unwell," after a meeting in June 1995.[1] Jerrold Post, formerly of the Central Intelligence Agency, deems him "seriously ill"[2] and Israeli military intelligence concludes that Assad "functions properly, is lucid and healthy," but that "he suffers from some basic diseases" (not further elaborated).[3]

What if Assad were to die tomorrow? What would happen? Before taking up these questions, a caution needs to be sounded. Outsiders have several times already prematurely ended Assad's rule. Sometimes they pointed to his political weakness: the British and American press in early 1980 ran a flurry of headlines like "Time Runs Out for Assad," "Crumbling Regime in Syria," and "Bleak Future for Assad Regime."[4] At other times, analysts buried the man alive. Writing in 1985, Alasdair Drysdale predicted that Assad's poor health meant that "the succession question is bound to resurface" before the end of his presidential term in 1992.[5] Reports of Assad's failing health then surfaced in October 1986, March 1987, June 1987, and January 1993. Assad lives on in 1995, very much in charge. These predictions suggest prudence when expecting an imminent end to the Assad era.

In the past, Assad tried without success to position two close relatives (his brother and his son) to succeed him. Rif'at al-Assad, Hafez's younger brother by seven years, was the heir apparent until he and several leading generals took advantage of the president's illness in November 1983 to make a play for power by deploying his troops, the Defense Companies, in Damascus. The venture failed and a few months later Hafez sent Rif'at into a gilded exile in Western Europe that lasted until the death of their mother in July 1992. Though he still holds the title of vice president—one of three such dignitaries—Rif'at no longer has a known power base; one Jordanian analyst went so far as to declare him "out of the running" in the succession game.[6]

Politics of Change in the Middle East (Boulder, CO: Westview, 1993), 16.

[1] *Jerusalem Post International Edition*, November 5, 1994; see also *Jerusalem Report*, July 27, 1995.

[2] *Philadelphia Inquirer*, October 28, 1994.

[3] Uri Saguy, head of Israeli military intelligence, *Yedi'ot Ahronot*, September 14, 1993.

[4] *Economist*, March 22, 1980; see also *Foreign Report*, March 26, 1980; and *Impact International*, April 11, 1980.

[5] Alasdair Drysdale, "The Succession Question in Syria," *Middle East Journal*, (Spring 1985): 257.

[6] Shakir al-Jawhari, *al-Dustur* (Amman), September 12, 1994.

Around 1986, Assad appointed his then twenty-four-year-old son Basil (born March 23, 1962) as security officer of the Presidential Palace, a move widely understood as the first step in preparing him for succession. Basil served in 1987 as his father's intermediary to Rif'at and became commander of the Defense Companies a year later. Basil's profile rose during the presidential referendum of 1991, when crowds chanted songs of support for him and vehicles from the army and secret police sported large color portraits of him. For the first time, Hafez al-Assad styled himself Abu Basil ("Father of Basil," a familiar term of address). A few weeks after the referendum, Staff Major Engineer Paratrooper Basil al-Assad embarked on his first diplomatic mission, traveling to Saudi Arabia to meet King Fahd. On other occasions, he stood in at official functions for his absent father. In June 1992, a Jordanian weekly reported that Assad had taken formal steps to make Basil his successor, calling it "almost certain" that Assad "has settled once and for all the issue of succession by . . . giving his son Basil major powers to decide Syrian internal and military affairs."[1]

These speculations came to an end on January 21, 1994, when Basil was killed in an accident while driving at high speed to the Damascus airport for a skiing trip abroad. The foreign minister, defense minister, and chief of staff comprised the delegation that went to Assad's residence to inform him of the tragedy. In his eulogy of thirty-one-year-old Basil, Hafez al-Assad called his death a "national loss" and the media repeated his words without cease.[2] A typical magazine article ("Basil al-Assad, the Golden Knight who Dismounted") deemed the young man's death "a national loss and the calamity that makes our hearts bleed."[3] A vast ritual of mourning for Basil then ensued. The entirety of Syria closed down in mourning, as did much of Lebanon (where radio stations switched to dirge music for three days). An eyewitness account from Damascus three weeks after Basil's death reported that on the streets of Damascus, "one can still see black mourning flags and long black streamers hanging down the facades of buildings while tens of thousands of pictures of Basil are on almost every wall."[4]

Over a year later, the mourning remained frenzied. Pictures remained ubiquitous, appearing not just on walls, cars and in stores, but also on such artifacts as dishes, clothing, and watches. Basil's pictures may, in fact, outnumber those of his father. All over Syria, places and institutions were renamed after the deceased. News reports

---

[1] *Akhbar al-Usbu'* (Amman), June 25, 1992.

[2] Syrian Arab Television, March 7, 1994.

[3] "Basil al-Asad al-Faris al-Dhahabi alladhi Tarajjal," *al-Manar al-Huda*, February 1994. The press habitually called Basil the "Golden Knight," a reference to his many equestrian triumphs (all of which took place, it bears noting, within Syria).

[4] *Jordan Times*, February 15, 1994.

mentioned farmers participating in "Martyr Staff Major Engineer Basil al-Assad studies" and the Ba'th Party indoctrinating youths in the "Basil al-Assad Course."[1]

This two-state effort to console a mourning father points to Assad's dashed political ambitions for his eldest son. Basil may have been eight years too young to meet Syria's constitutional requirements to serve as president, but that hardly mattered; in Assad's Syria, effective power does not require holding high office (as Basil's career already showed, undertaking important diplomatic missions in his capacity as a staff major). Basil's military service, his reported anti-drug efforts, diplomatic missions, and acceptability to leading regime figures presumably would have prepared him to take over upon his father's demise.

Almost immediately following Basil's death, the elder Assad recruited his next son, the twenty-nine year-old Bashshar, to follow in Basil's steps. Bashshar, shy, soft-spoken, and apolitical, returned from his ophthalmology studies in London to enroll in Syria's military academy. Upon graduating in November 1994, he become Captain Dr. Bashshar, commanding officer of a brigade in the Republican Guard, the force that protects the president. He quickly assumed other of his late brother's duties, such as fighting corruption, undertaking diplomatic missions, meeting foreign leaders, and appearing by his father's side at formal events. (In addition, Mahir, a third son, also became an officer in the Republican Guard.) At the same time, in a rare public interview, he disavowed any intention to take power, expressing both deep respect for the constitution (a "sacred" document) which stipulates a minimum age of forty and declaring his father to be "at the peak of his activity and political presence."[2]

Bashshar's complete inexperience may open the way for the re-emergence of Rif'at as the leading family contender; it also may provide an opportunity for the Alawi barons to stake out a place for themselves in the succession battle. In any case, not the Ba'th Party, but the Group that surrounds Assad will probably have the decisive say about Assad's successor. Its importance in determining power in post-Assad Syria at least partially explains why the president engaged in a dramatic series of personnel changes shortly after Basil's death. Several long-standing aides lost their positions in 1994, including: 'Ali Haydar, commander of the Special Forces; Majid Sa'id, head of the General Intelligence Directorate; and 'Ali Malahafji, commander of the Air Force. Removing these Alawi heavyweights and replacing them with younger, less established men will presumably make it easier for

---

[1] Syrian Arab Television, January 14, 1995; see also Syrian Arab Republic Radio, August 10, 1995.

[2] *Al-Muharrir*, July 31, 1995. Bashshar put in an interesting cameo appearance as an eight-year-old in Richard Nixon, *Memoirs* (New York: Grosset & Dunlap, 1978), 1013.

Bashshar to establish himself as a force in Syria politics. Much depends on how long Hafez lives; and the capabilities that Bashshar shows for politics.

In the end, however, the very nature of the Assad regime makes it unlikely that its head will be able securely to bequeath his kingdom to a relative or a clansman. Twentieth-century history suggests that when ideology, ethnicity, and family all play a role, the result is too volatile to plan or predict. No one knows what will happen after Assad's death.

IV   ELEMENTS OF A BACKLASH STATE

[Assad] made himself felt on the world stage at a time when all the others were shaking their heads and accepting whatever came their way.

—'Imad Fawzi Shu'aybi[1]

With the Soviet captain gone and the team disbanded, Assad finds himself on his own. He has come to terms with the West's predominance, helping in the Kuwait crisis and taking part in the Arab-Israeli peace process; but even as he does so, he maintains his distance from it and retains close links to an anti-Western network. More than any other former member of the Soviet bloc, Assad keeps his options open, ready to go the West's way if the timing and the price are right, against it if not, or both ways at once.

This points to a larger pattern: Assad persistently plays a double game, not committing one way or another, doing two things at once, holding out for a better opportunity later.[2] In the wake of the Soviet collapse, he turns toward the West while still maintaining his anti-Western credentials and many of his old activities.

Rogue Activities

Damascus has not abandoned tactics honed during years of Syrian-Soviet partnership. It provides sanctuary to Western criminals, assists terrorist organizations, traffics in drugs, and forges dollar bills.

Sanctuary to criminals. Western criminals, especially fanatical Germans, frequently find safe haven in Syria. Aloïs Brunner—SS *Obersturmbannführer*, Adolph Eichmann's closest collaborator, inventor of the mobile extermination unit, a man responsible for implementing the deaths of at least 120,000 Jews plus others, and in Simon Wiesenthal's estimation "the worst ever" of the Third Reich

---

[1] 'Imad Fawzi Shu'aybi, "Risala Maftuha," *al-Diyar*, June 7, 1994.

[2] See, for example, Daniel Pipes, "Understanding Asad," *Middle East Quarterly* (December 1994): 51-52.

criminals[1]—is the most infamous of this group; he has evidently lived in Damascus since 1954. In addition to the two French courts that sentenced Brunner to death *in absentia* in 1955, international warrants for his arrest have been issued by German courts in 1961 and 1984, by Interpol in 1986, and again by French courts in 1988 and 1991. The Syrian authorities deny Brunner's presence in their country, saying that he exists only in their critics' imagination. When confronted by foreign diplomats with information about Brunner's residence,[2] Foreign Minister al-Sharaa asked with indignation how they could "believe a journalist and not a government."[3]

According to French sources, Brunner died in the summer of 1992; Simon Wiesenthal says he has left Syria, perhaps for a remote area of northern Argentina. If so, he left behind numerous spiritual heirs. Ilich Ramírez Sánchez ("Carlos the Jackal"), for many years the world's most notorious terrorist, arrived in Syria sometime in 1984-85 and stayed about nine years.[4] As soon as Magdelena Kopp of the Baader-Meinhof gang left a French prison in May 1985, she went directly to Damascus, where she married Carlos. Bruno Bréguet, her Swiss associate, also headed for Damascus. Johannes Weinrich, Carlos's top aide, at some point joined them there.

Other terrorist luminaries who have made their home in Syria or the Bekaa Valley include: Frédéric Oriach of Action Direct;[5] Kozo

---

[1] *New York Times*, May 31, 1991. Serge Klarsfeld calls him "the last one who escaped" of the major Nazi war criminals (*Jerusalem Post International Edition*, March 3, 1990). Mary Felstiner, an American historian who studied Brunner's role in the Holocaust, says that "Genocide was his sole passion" (*Reader's Digest*, June 1990).

[2] Individuals who made contact with Brunner include Beate Klarsfeld, the Nazi hunter (who in 1981 confirmed his presence in Damascus with a telephone call to his apartment); a reporter for the *Chicago Sun-Times* did likewise in October 1987. Two German journalists met Brunner and took a series of color pictures of him in his Damascus neighborhood and on the beach to prove the encounter ("Damaskus, Rue Haddad Nummer 7," *Bunte*, December 1985, 16-27); Didier Epelbaum ("Brunner est à Damas," *Le Monde*, January 18, 1992) provides the names of many more individuals, including ex-Nazis, who have testified about Brunner living in Damascus and concludes that the evidence is too diverse for "a shadow of a doubt to exist" about Brunner's whereabouts.

[3] *Le Monde*, December 21, 1991. Curiously, Sharaa used precisely the same argument on the subject of PKK leader Abdullah Öcalan, characterizing press accounts about his living in Damascus as "fictitious reports and phony photographs" (*Hürriyet*, August 23, 1994).

[4] Carlos's extradition from the Sudan to France in August 1994 prompted far-ranging and contradictory speculations, many of them concerning Syria. In the main, they held that the Syrian state deported Carlos (*al-Sharq al-Awsat*, August 18, 1994); or that it informed either the Sudanese (*Libération*, August 17, 1994) or a Western government (*Jerusalem Report*, September 8, 1994) of Carlos's whereabouts, thereby hoping to get Damascus off the U.S. government's list of states supporting terrorism (*Jerusalem Post International Edition*, September 3, 1994).

[5] Charles Villeneuve and Jean-Pierre Péret, *Histoire Secrète du Terrorisme: Les Juges de l'impossible* (Paris: Plon, 1987), 184; Annie Laurent and Antoine Basbous, *Guerres secrètes*

Okamoto of the Japanese Red Army, who helped kill twenty-four passengers at the Tel Aviv airport in 1972 and turned up in the Bekaa after his 1985 release from prison; and Murtaza Bhutto, son of Zulfikar and younger brother of Benazir, who avoided arrest in Pakistan for his involvement in a 1978 hijacking by living in Syria until October 1993. Erich Honecker did not take up the Syrians' 1992 offer to move to Damascus, choosing Chile instead, where he died in 1994.

Terrorism. Along with a few other Middle East leaders, Assad transformed terrorism, long the method of fugitive revolutionaries, into a powerful instrument of state power. In recognition of Syrian behavior, the U.S. government in 1979 made Syria a charter member of its list of states that support terrorism, a status which it continues to enjoy.

Syrian officials sometimes dismiss the listing as trivial. "We don't care about this list," the foreign minister says, "We don't believe in it."[1] At other times they express outrage at Washington, and in so doing offer some novel and interesting arguments. Assad defines the terrorist as "a criminal who kills for the sake of stealing, plundering, blackmailing and in a general manner, for evil personal reasons."[2] At other times, he turns the argument around, saying that if a Palestinian fighting the Israeli occupation is a terrorist, so then was George Washington. Assad's definitions imply, of course, that the Syrian state supports no terrorists.

A more conventional definition[3] reveals quite a different pattern. According to L. Paul Bremer III, head of counterterrorism for the Department of State in 1986-89, "Five or six of the world's most dangerous terrorist groups have their headquarters in Damascus."[4] Abdullah Öcalan, leader of the Kurdish PKK organization, stated in 1991 that Damascus supports some seventy-two other organizations such as his own; a year later, he counted seventy such organizations in Lebanon and fifty in Syria.[5] Israeli sources estimate that 1,200 terrorists rely on Syrian support, as well as many others who provide them with

---

au Liban (Paris: Gallimard, 1987), 327; *Le Nouvel Observateur*, September 19, 1986; *L' Événement du Jeudi*, September 18-24, 1986.

[1] Faruq al-Sharaa, *New York Times*, December 10, 1993.

[2] Syrian Arab Television, October 2, 1993.

[3] This author's favorite definition, by Alex P. Schmid, notes that "Terrorists have elevated practices which are excesses of war to the level of routine tactics" and defines terrorism as the "peacetime equivalent of war crimes." In Alex P. Schmid and Ronald D. Crelinsten, eds., *Western Responses to Terrorism* (London: Frank Cass, 1993), 12. Rebeh Kebir, chairman of the Executive Committee of the Islamic Salvation Front (FIS) has offered an Islamic counterpart to this, deeming terrorism "any action that violates the *sharia*" (*al-Hayat*, June 19, 1995).

[4] L. Paul Bremer III, "Iran and Syria—Keep the Bums Out," *New York Times*, December 17, 1991.

[5] *Milliyet*, March 23, 1991 and March 26, 1992; see also *Ikibin'e Doğru*, March 22, 1992. *Al-Ahram*, July 18, 1995, counted thirty-seven opposition groups based in Syria.

services; Turkish eye-witnesses say that the PKK alone has some 500 armed fighters.[1]

Since the mid-1980s, Syrian tactics of terrorism have evolved. The government then got directly involved in terrorist acts, notably in 1986 when Nizar al-Hindawi, a Syrian agent, attempted to blow up an El Al aircraft leaving London. In recent years, Damascus has been more cautious and no longer relies on its own personnel; instead, it works with like-minded terrorist organizations operating in the Middle East and thc West, giving them safe-haven and much other support. This terrorism by proxy permits the Syrians to establish a wall of deniability, so that they reap the political benefits of terrorism without paying the full political price for its sponsorship. As for the terrorist groups, they benefit by gaining vastly enhanced funding, intelligence, training, and weaponry; they also win access to diplomatic pouches and to alliances with like-minded organizations.

Terrorist organizations operating from Syria or Syrian-controlled territory in Lebanon, past and present, fall under five main rubrics:

(1) Palestinian: the ten groups in the National, Democratic, and Islamic Front, a loose alliance of rejectionists opposed to the Israeli-Palestinian peace process (see Appendix I), as well as some related organizations.

(2) Lebanese: Hezbollah and its affiliates (such as the Islamic Jihad Organization in Lebanon), the Syrian Social Nationalist Party, the Ba'th Party of Lebanon, the Lebanese Revolutionary Brigades, and the Lebanese Armed Revolutionary Faction (FARL).

(3) Turkish: the Revolutionary Left (Devrimci Sol, known as Dev-Sol) on the left and the Gray Wolves on the right; the Worker's Party of Kurdistan (PKK); and the Armenian Secret Army for the Liberation of Armenia (ASALA).

(4) Other Middle Eastern and Muslim: Arab Egypt, the Committee for the Defense of Democratic Liberties in Jordan, Polisario (Western Sahara), the Democratic Front for the Liberation of Somalia, the Eritrean Liberation Front, Zulfikar (Pakistan), the Pattani United Liberation Organization (Thailand), and Abu Sayyaf (Philippines).

(5) Non-Middle Eastern and non-Muslim: the Red Army Faction of West Germany, Action Direct of France, the Red Brigades of Italy, the Basque ETA, the Fighting Communist Cells of Belgium, the Liberation Tigers of Tamil Eelam of Sri Lanka, and the Japanese Red Army.

Since 1991, Assad has somewhat reduced his regime's active support for terrorist groups. It appears that he closed two camps in Lebanon belonging to the Fatah Revolutionary Council of Abu Nidal (Sabri al-Banna), and may have forced Carlos to leave the country, starting a chain of events that eventually led to the Sudanese authorities handing Carlos over to France in August 1994 to stand trial.

---

[1] *Ha'aretz*, December 23, 1991; see also *Jerusalem Report*, March 19, 1992.

Also, after hosting Weinrich for some years in Syria, beyond the reach of repeated German efforts to extradite him, Assad had him leave as well; in June 1995 the Yemeni authorities extradited him to Germany where he will stand trial. These two court cases should reveal much about the Syrian role in terrorism.

Syrian-sponsored groups continue to target Turkish and Israeli interests, usually in their home countries but also abroad (PKK attacks on Turkish embassies in Europe, Hezbollah's attack on Israeli and Jewish targets in Buenos Aires, Argentina).[1] Terrorist leaders such as Palestinian leader Ahmad Jibril and George Habash move about Damascus freely (foreigners sometimes spot them at the Sheraton Hotel) and periodically meet with senior Syrian officials. Responsibility for terrorist acts committed in Israel by Islamic Jihad or Hamas is often claimed by those groups' political headquarters in Damascus. Syrian behavior has slightly improved, but the terrorist dossiers remain open.

Drug cultivation and trafficking. As with terrorism, Syria belongs to a select list of states identified by the U.S. government as unhelpful in prosecuting the campaign against drug trafficking. (The other current members are Burma, Iran, and Nigeria). Syrian profits from drugs have two main sources: narco-terrorism and Lebanon.

Terrorist groups often rely on drug trafficking to pay for their operations, and those based in Syria fit this pattern. Fevzi Acıkgöz, for example, a high-ranking defector from the PKK, testified about his experience in 1989 carrying drug money to Syria:

> I carried 7 million Deutsche marks, entrusted to me by a PKK representative before I flew directly from Frankfurt to Damascus. The guards in the airport in Syria stopped me, but when they found out who I was, I was led past the controls. Most of the money was to be delivered to Hafez al-Assad's regime. The Syrian state earns a lot of money from these kinds of contributions from a number of illegal organizations.[2]

An Israeli police source similarly described Syria's drug operations in Lebanon. At the acme, Minister of Defense Mustafa Tallas sells permits to grow drugs for about $1,000 to each of a thousand farmers.

> A low-ranking Syrian army man controls each village. Groups of villages are controlled by officers with the rank of captain or major, while larger areas are overseen by lieutenant colonels or brigadier generals. The Syrian fee for

---

[1]   On the possible Syrian hand in the July 1994 bombing of the Jewish cultural center in Buenos Aires, see *El Periodico* (Barcelona), September 25, 1994.

[2]   *Weekendavisen* (Copenhagen), June 3-9, 1994, translated and reprinted in the *Turkish Times*, August 15, 1994; In a subsequent account, Acıkgöz told of carrying the money in his bag, of being "led around" the border controls and driven in a Mercedes to Öcalan's apartment, then spending the night there (*Weekendavisen*, July 8-14, 1994). Another report, based on Turkish intelligence sources, estimates the PKK's annual drug sales at DM 500 million and controlling a majority of the German market (*Turkish Daily News*, July 11, 1995).

> growing opium on each dunam is $25-$50 a year, thus even a medium-sized village with 4,000 dunams means profits to the Syrians of $100,000 to $200,000 annually.[1]

Many official U.S. sources have cited official Syrian participation in the drug trade out of Lebanon. A 1989 Drug Enforcement Agency report estimated that Syrian officials take in at least half of the $700 million to $1 billion in profits associated with Lebanon's drug trade. A 1991 House Republican Research Committee report notes that "the highest levels of the Syrian government are directly involved in the production, processing, and distribution of drugs throughout the West." A December 1992 report of the House Judiciary Subcommittee on Crime and Criminal Justice pointed to the huge growth in the Lebanese drug trade under Syrian auspices. In 1976 the arable land in the Bekaa Valley devoted to drugs came to just 10 percent; when the report was written, it had reached 90 percent. The report not only points out the participation of top Syrian officials in trafficking drugs, but it lists names at the highest levels of Syrian politics: Ghazi Kan'an, the effective head of the Syrian occupation in Lebanon; 'Ali Duba, head of the Military Intelligence Department; Mustafa Tallas, defense minister; and Rif'at al-Assad, brother of the president. Another U.S. government report estimated that over a quarter of the heroin entering the United States comes from Syrian-controlled regions of Lebanon. The 1995 edition of the State Department's annual narcotics survey states that

> Syria is an important transit point for narcotics flowing through the Middle East to Europe and, to a lesser extent, the U.S. regional heroin and hashish trafficking networks. . . . [T]he flow of narcotics did not diminish in 1994. . . . Credible reports to Syrian military protection for drug traffickers persisted in 1994, despite official claims to the contrary.[2]

Starting in 1991, the Syrians claimed some impressive figures for drugs seized (e.g., 491,231 kilograms of hashish, 25,747 kilograms of heroin, and 2,134 kilograms of cocaine in just the first quarter of 1992)[3] and some large-scale crop burnings in Lebanon. Western journalists came away with decidedly contrary views of these efforts in 1992. The *Christian Science Monitor*'s Jim Muir deems the crackdown "much more serious than ever before," but Joseph Matar and Jonathan Broder of the *Jerusalem Report* dub the effort merely "a more serious show than usual." Two British periodicals diverge even more radically; the *Financial Times* asserts that opium and cannabis production in the Bekaa Valley "has been wiped out by the Syrian army," but *Foreign*

---

[1]   Rafi Peled, *Jerusalem Post*, September 14, 1991.

[2]   Department of State, *International Narcotics Control Strategy Report* (Washington, DC: U.S. Government Printing Office, 1995), 441-42.

[3]   *Tishrin*, June 30, 1992.

Report claims that "most of the fields burned contain nothing more forbidden than wheat stubble."[1] In its *International Narcotics Control Strategy Report*, the U.S. government indicates a major reduction of Lebanon's opium production but a booming cannabis trade.

If Damascus does get serious about drug cultivation in Lebanon, the decision may result less from a wish to please the West than from alarm at the spread of addiction in Syria itself. The Department of State tells of "anecdotal evidence of increased drug use among well-to-do young people,"[2] a trend that could one day harm the regime.

Counterfeiting. The Syrians (perhaps in cooperation with Iran) have produced and distributed $2 billion-$3 billion of counterfeit U.S. currency in the past two years. The "Supernote" appears to be manufactured in Syria or in Syrian-controlled Lebanon, in large facilities by Syrian soldiers. The total amount in circulation may reach $4 billion. Robert Kupperman of the Center for Strategic and International Studies calls the Supernote "the most nearly perfect $100 bills that the U.S. Secret Service has ever detected."[3] Their numbers and quality are wrecking minor havoc. Reports from Europe and East Asia claim that retailers and even bankers are refusing $100 bills. In Jordan moneychangers sent out special warnings in April 1994 against accepting forgeries. Even in the United States, the Supernote fools the currency scanners at the Federal Reserve banks. It's no wonder that the Secret Service reports seizing only $121 million in counterfeit notes outside the United States in the course of an entire year.

The counterfeiters' motives—beyond making money—are the subject of some speculation. A Senate staffer sees this as the way for Damascus to pay for a nuclear facility. Others see it as an attack on the U.S. financial system; indeed, according to Frederic Dannen and Ira Silverman, the problem has already reached such proportions that "it has begun to undermine confidence in United States currency."[4] Paul Kelly, the Federal prosecutor in Boston who dealt with the Supernote problem, thinks the goal might be nothing less than "to destabilize the economy of the United States."[5]

In response, the Treasury has set up an office in Cyprus and radically overhauled the $100 bill, hoping to make it more difficult to forge; changes include: moving the portrait to the side, implanting holograms, adding watermarks to the paper, and adding colors. Secretary of State Christopher reportedly brought up this topic in a

---

[1] *Christian Science Monitor*, August 7, 1992; see also *Jerusalem Report*, July 30, 1992; *Financial Times*, July 8, 1992; and *Foreign Report*, December 12, 1991.

[2] Department of State, *International Narcotics*, 443.

[3] *Washington Post*, April 8, 1994; *Coin World*, July 27, 1992.

[4] Frederic Dannen and Ira Silverman, "The Supernote," *The New Yorker*, October 23, 1995.

[5] Quoted in Dannen and Silverman, "The Supernote."

May 1994 meeting with Hafez al-Assad, but he lacked specific information about the production facilities whereabouts, and so made no headway.

Non-Western Connections

Assad goes to some pains to maintain ties with former and present opponents of the West, presumably in the hopes of minimizing his dependence on the West and so retaining maximum freedom of maneuver.

Former opponents means the ex-Soviet bloc. Somewhere between a thousand and 2,400 technicians from Russia and Eastern Europe still work in Syria (down from about 8,700 in 1988), where they retain key roles in government enterprises. Indeed, maintaining some of Syria's infrastructure (roads, sewage, irrigation) depends on their expertise. On signing a wide range of bilateral agreements in April 1994, the Russian first deputy prime minister recalled the "old and long-lasting ties" between the two sides and deemed it a "duty" to promote and enhance those ties in the future.[1] Alexander Bovin, Russia's ambassador to Israel, separately characterized those ties as "not so tight as they were before. But in general they are very intense" and claimed that Moscow has at least as much influence on Syria as does Washington.[2]

Over the years, Damascus worked up a huge debt to the Soviet Union for weapons purchases and other benefits, variously estimated between $10 billion and $19 billion.[3] Of this, Russia's share makes up a large majority; $11 billion is a commonly cited figure. Reports in May 1994 indicated that Moscow wrote off $10 billion of that amount, at the same time that it contracted to sell about $500 million in armaments to Syria on a cash basis.

Noting that the Syrian government yet depends heavily on specialists from the former Soviet bloc to help with many projects, Fred H. Lawson concludes that Damascus "has little incentive to abandon its established relations with the East and turn permanently to the West."[4] But these are former opponents: the Russian government apparently pressured Assad to meet with Israel's Rabin, or at least to have their foreign ministers (at the time Peres and Sharaa) meet—something inconceivable in the Soviet era.

---

[1]   Oleg Soskovets, on Syrian Arab Republic Radio, April 28, 1994.

[2]   *Jerusalem Post International Edition*, November 26, 1994.

[3]   Andre Volpin of the Moscow Institute of Oriental Studies (quoted in the *Washington Times*, June 11, 1993) gives an $8 billion figure for just Russia; Anthony H. Cordesman and Abraham R. Wagner suggest $19 billion for the Soviet Union in *The Lessons of Modern War: The Arab-Israeli Conflicts 1973-1989*, vol. 1, (Boulder, CO: Westview, 1990), 276.

[4]   Fred H. Lawson, "Domestic Transformation and Foreign Steadfastness in Contemporary Syria," *Middle East Journal* 48 (Winter 1994): 48.

Present opponents means states both in the Middle East (Iran, Libya) and outside it (China, North Korea, Cuba). While China and North Korea provide Syria with small amounts of economic assistance and military supplies, Iran is clearly the key to this network. The Iran-Syria alliance took shape soon after Khomeini came to power in February 1979 and acquired operational form when the Iraq-Iran war began in September 1980. For years, the two states cooperated in the first place against Iraq, but also as rejectionists in the Arab-Israeli conflict and as quasi-allies in Lebanon. They established important military, trade, and even touristic relations. The alliance has had a surprisingly durable quality given the two sides' many differences, from the ideological (Ba'thist vs. fundamentalist Muslim) to the ethnic (who should control three small islands in the Persian Gulf, Arabs or Iranians). The two states have institutionalized their relations (a joint commission meets every six months, for example, to foster cooperation). "Iran is a friend," Vice President 'Abd al-Halim Khaddam says, "and our relations with it are more than good."[1] There is no reason to disbelieve him.

Military Buildup

Assad's military power continues to grow. Syria has one of the largest armies in the Middle East, the largest tank corps, and the largest stockpile of chemical weapons. Since the end of the Kuwait War, it has deployed a new armored division and is in the process of forming a brigade outfitted with Scud-C missiles that can reach most of Israel's population. Damascus appears to be near to engineering deadly poisonous anthrax viral agents into weapons and is starting nuclear research. In all, according to Israeli intelligence sources, Damascus has spent $1.4 billion on military modernization efforts since the Kuwait War. As in years past, the Syrian regime spends nearly half of its budget[2] and most of its foreign aid on military-related items. The new development is that Damascus now earns over $2 billion annually in hard currency profits from oil sales.

Assad seems to have learned two main military lessons from the Kuwait War: advanced fighter aircraft can elude or defeat any of the older generation of radar and missile technologies, and surface-to-surface missiles provide Arab leaders with important benefits when used against Israel—adulation on the Arab street, possible Israeli passivity, and virtual invulnerability from Western search-and-destroy missions. These two insights prompted Assad to use most of the more than $2 billion windfall Syria's government received for its stance in the Kuwait War to buy state-of-the-art fighter aircraft, anti-aircraft systems, and surface-to-surface missiles.

---

[1] *Al-Safir*, July 10, 1995.

[2] *Defense News*, July 4-10, 1994.

Conventional weapons came mostly from Syria's traditional sources. Western intelligence agencies estimated that in 1991 the Syrians contracted for a long list of weapons from Russia: forty-eight MIG-29 jet fighters, twenty-four Sukhoy-24 low-altitude bombers, three hundred T-72 tanks, and a number of SAM-11 and SAM-13 missiles. In early 1992, the Syrians reportedly acquired another twenty-four MIG-29s, another three hundred T-72 tanks, and unspecified numbers of SAM-10s (which resemble the Patriot) and SAM-16s (like the Stinger). In April 1994, the Russian and Syrian governments signed a military and technical agreement, thought to be their first in the post-Soviet era; but, bowing to new sensibilities, it covers only "defensive weapons and spare parts."[1] Two months later, there were reports of Russian sales of anti-tank and radar systems to Syria. About the same time, the Russian chief of staff visited Damascus, signed a dozen agreements, and called his visit "a new starting point in Russian-Syrian military cooperation."[2] The Russian ambassador raised the possibility of selling an air defense system to Syria. Russia once again became Syria's main arms supplier.[3]

The Syrians approached other states for arms, including Slovakia (250 advanced tanks), India (T-72 tanks and MIG-29 fighters) and Germany (mechanisms to extend the range of Scud missiles). In one puzzling transaction, the Pakistani government ostensibly gave six of its domestically-made Mashshaq aircraft to Syria as part of a "gift package."[4] The Kuwait War also produced weapons from unexpected sources; Syria's Ninth Division returned home with dozens of operational Iraqi tanks, and other units brought back U.S.-made armored vehicles.

Assad appears to have also decided that the extinction of his Soviet patron requires him to find new forms of strategic insurance against Israel. The evidence suggests that this means not just some sixty-two launchers and hundreds of surface-to-surface missiles but also the means to produce missiles within Syria. Ballistic missiles first reached Syria in 1974 and have steadily increased in numbers and quality over the next two decades. At first, the Soviet Union provided most of the armaments; since 1988, Syria has looked increasingly to North Korea and China for missiles. Still the Russians retain a role: after the U.S.

---

[1] *Al-Sharq al-Awsat*, April 29, 1994. "Defensive" weapons can, of course, include almost anything in the arsenal. Spare parts, however, pose a particularly acute problem for Syria because its sources in the former Soviet states do not produce these reliably and the consequences could be severe in time of war.

[2] Russian Armed Forces Chief of Staff Mikhail Petrovich Kolesnikov on Radio Monte Carlo, June 8, 1994.

[3] Not every weapon contracted for from Russia will reach Syria, however. The two governments have not yet settled the issue of Syrian debt and until they do, new deliveries will remain problematic.

[4] Pakistani Television (Islamabad), October 4, 1994.

Navy nearly intercepted a shipment of Korean missiles to Syria via Iran in March 1992, Russian transport planes in August 1993 ferried a shipment of Scud-Cs to Syria.[1]

As for producing its own missiles, Damascus apparently reached an agreement with Beijing in November 1991 to build two plants in Syria, in Aleppo and south of Hama. What these plants manufacture is unclear: sources variously reported it was liquid fuel for Scud missiles, whole M-9 type missiles, or guidance systems for unspecified missiles. In December, word of the North Koreans helping build a Scud-C missile factory leaked out. In May 1992, news came out of Iran that four Syrians had been accidentally killed while working on a project to extend the range of Scud missiles,[2] followed in August 1992 by news of a plant in Syria to manufacture solid fuel for M-9 missiles. Israel's Prime Minister Rabin announced in June 1994 that Syria had just acquired the means to produce surface-to-surface missiles, and commented that their quality made the Iraqi Scuds of the Kuwait War mere "child's play."[3]

Assad first acquired chemical weapons shortly after reaching power and developed the means to manufacture chemical agents in 1985. Today, the country is self-sufficient in chemical production. Chemical bombs and warheads appear mainly to be intended for use against Israeli population centers, either to threaten retaliation or to impede the mobilization of troops. Syria currently produces hundreds of metric tons of chemical weapons annually and disposes of a mighty chemical arsenal.

Damascus has also sought a biological weapons capability. The Syrians ordered forty-five tons of trimethyl phosphite, a key ingredient in nerve gas, from an Indian source and took possession of half of it in 1992. (The second half was intercepted by the U.S. and German governments.) Equipment ordered from Baxter International, an American company, was apparently intended for manufacturing biological agents.[4]

As for nuclear weapons, here too the Soviet collapse appears to have shifted Assad's approach. Long diffident about playing this game, he has since 1988 been starting to put together a civilian nuclear program that could later serve as the basis for building nuclear weapons. Though stymied by lack of funds and International Atomic Energy Agency (IAEA) restrictions (which may have blocked the Chinese from selling a nuclear reactor to Syria in early 1992), public announcements and unofficial reports point to a Syrian intent on gaining expertise and developing infrastructure. The sense that Assad

---

[1] IDF Radio, August 15, 1993.

[2] *Sunday Telegraph*, May 31, 1992.

[3] Israel Television, June 22, 1994.

[4] *Insight*, August 30, 1993.

had made the decision to go for nuclear arms grew stronger with reports in mid-1995 about Syrian efforts to buy from Argentina a five-megawatt nuclear reactor operating on enriched uranium, along with ancillary equipment, ostensibly for research purposes.[1]

Syrian forces have engaged in impressive military buildups several times before (after the 1967, 1973, and 1982 wars, for instance) but the post-1991 effort has been unprecedented in terms of size, quality, and reach; for the first time, Syrian armaments challenge not just the Israel Defense Forces but Israel's civilian population. Israeli analysts concluded by late 1991 that the Syrian military had attained a stronger position *vis-à-vis* Israel than ever before. In 1994, Israel's prime minister stated (with perhaps a dose of hyperbole) he "could not remember such a large quantity of arms reaching Syria, and of the most advanced type."[2]

Of course, Israel's forces did not stand still in this period; an assessment of the military balance shows that, in all, Israel gained relative to Syria and could defeat any Syrian offensive. The Syrian strategy of targeting Israeli civilians implicitly acknowledged this assessment: unable to plan for victory, Damascus decided to make warfare unbearably costly for Israel—an essentially defensive posture.

Viewed in its totality, the Syrian military buildup appears to serve several purposes. First, it is key to Syria's pretensions to regional great power status. By 1993, Damascus had, according to Michael Eisenstadt, "the most advanced strategic weapons capability in the Arab world."[3] This muscle provides Assad with a military option—especially *vis-à-vis* his weaker neighbors (Lebanon, Jordan) but also with regard to his more powerful ones (Iraq, Turkey).

Second, the arsenal keeps alive a military option against Israel. Conventional wisdom holds that, at this point, "Syria has no military option" and that it has "no chance at all" of recovering the Golan Heights through military action.[4] But matters are not so simple. A protracted war with Israel is probably more than the Syrians can handle, but they could mount a limited strike on the Golan, either to seize it outright (their strategy in 1973) or to provoke the great powers to take diplomatic action (the Egyptian strategy in 1973). Indeed, the 1973 campaign remains a model for recovering the Golan; Eisenstadt

---

[1] *Yedi'ot Ahronot,* July 14, 1995. On a visit to Israel, Argentina's Foreign Minister Guido Di Tella agreed not to sell the reactor to Syria before it signed a peace treaty with Israel. See *Ha'aretz,* July 20, 1995; and Kol Yisra'el, July 23, 1995.

[2] Yitzhak Rabin, Kol Yisra'el, June 28, 1994.

[3] Michael Eisenstadt, "Syria's Strategic Weapons," *Jane's Intelligence Review,* April 1993, 168.

[4] Thomas L. Friedman, "The Twilight Zone," *New York Times,* June 25, 1995; see also Alasdair Drysdale, "Syria since 1988: From Crisis to Opportunity," in Robert O. Freedman, ed., *The Middle East After Iraq's Invasion of Kuwait* (Gainesville: University Press of Florida, 1993), 285.

notes that "the Syrians have rehearsed updated and improved versions of the battle plan a number of times since then."[1]

Those who discount the possibility of a Syrian attack on Israel ought to recall the assessment given by the deputy head of Israeli army intelligence, Brig. Gen. Aryeh Shalev, on October 3, 1973, just three days before Syria's surprise attack on Israel:

> Assad is a realistic, cool and balanced leader. . . . Syria won't go to war by herself. Assad is scared the IDF will reach Damascus. War just wouldn't make sense, and the Syrian deployment is apparently only because of fear of Israeli attack. . . . [I]t is unlikely that a co-ordinated Egyptian-Syrian war will begin in the near future.[2]

Israel's former commander on the Golan front, Yitzhak Mordechai, publicly noted that Assad has the "capability, in a short period of time, to perpetrate a strategic fraud on Israel and, for the purpose of tactical surprise, [he] could launch powerful forces against the state."[3] Israeli Foreign Minister Ehud Barak, then Israel's chief of staff, flatly asserts that "from a technical-military point of view, [Damascus] has a military option" against Israel.[4]

Third, unconventional weaponry at least partially compensates for the loss of the Soviet umbrella. Should Israeli-Syrian negotiations collapse and Assad retreat to full-fledged rejectionism to undermine the remnants of the peace process, this arsenal would give Assad the option to join with other anti-Western states to challenge the West and threaten its friends (e.g., Jordan). Although Assad is yet far from possessing a nuclear capability, the temptation to seek it must be great for (as the North Korean example shows) the mere possibility of such power dramatically increases a state's leverage.

Aggressive Neighbor

At the height of the Cold War, when Syria was Moscow's most powerful Arab client, Damascus pursued a range of aggressive policies against the Palestinians and all of its neighbors but one—Iraq. Today, with Syria a coquettish participant in the peace process, eager to woo and be wooed by the United States, the edges have been rounded off of Syrian policy and its aggressive behavior has become more subtle and nuanced. Nevertheless, Damascus still maintains a policy of active or passive belligerence toward each of these five actors, plus Iraq.

---

[1] Michael Eisenstadt, *Arming for Peace: Syria's Elusive Quest for "Strategic Parity,"* Policy Paper Number Thirty-One (Washington, DC: The Washington Institute for Near East Policy, 1992), 16.

[2] Quoted in Moshe Ma'oz, *Assad, The Sphinx of Damascus: A Political Biography* (New York: Weidenfeld & Nicholson, 1988), 89-90.

[3] *Jerusalem Post International Edition*, September 10, 1994.

[4] *Al Hamishmar*, September 14, 1994. In the same interview, Barak concedes that Damascus "has a far smaller military option than in 1973."

Lebanon. Syrian soldiers entered Lebanon in large numbers in 1976 toward the start of the Lebanese civil war; despite the war's end and repeated promises to leave, 35,000 of them remain yet in Lebanon. While some analysts believe the troops will eventually have to leave, if only because of the military liability of spreading out the troops so widely,[1] the reasons to stay may be more compelling.

Ruling Lebanon serves several purposes for Assad. It marks a significant step toward bringing all of Greater Syria under Damascus's direct control. It permits the Syrians to stamp out press criticism and political intrigue that once came out of Beirut. Far from a financial liability, Lebanon provides Syrian officials with an annual income from drug trafficking estimated in the hundreds of millions of dollars. It also offers a convenient venue for keeping terrorist proxies under Syrian control but outside of direct Syrian responsibility.

In addition, the Lebanese theater provides Assad with an arena within which to tangle with Israel without endangering his own regime; the two sides have tacitly agreed to reserve total war for the Golan Heights and engage in only lesser skirmishes in Lebanon, preferably via proxies. (This policy explains why the Syrian president's Arab enemies ridicule him as "the lion [*asad*] of Lebanon and the rabbit [*arnab*] of Golan.")

Assad has many levers of power over Lebanon, especially since Damascus won legal status for its special role in the May 1991 Treaty of Brotherhood, Cooperation, and Coordination. Syrian troops engage in small-scale operations within the country more akin to police work than a military campaign, and even maintain a barracks inside the Lebanese defense ministry. Syrian intelligence agents keep up a formidable presence throughout Lebanon; according to *Foreign Report*, they even disguise themselves as fruit and vegetable vendors.[2]

These agents operate almost entirely outside the rule of law (routinely making arrests without warrants, for example), one of several aspects of Syrian activities there that led Human Rights Watch to conclude that "the record of violations in Syrian-controlled Lebanon has been worse than in Syria."[3] The deep infiltration of the *mukhabarat* in all spheres of Lebanese society suggests that even if Assad were to fulfill his obligations under the Ta'if Accord to withdraw Syrian troops from Beirut, he would still have enough assets left in Lebanon to exert considerable control over the country.

In fact, the Lebanese government is so subservient to Syrian wishes that Lebanese politicians travel to Damascus before making any major

---

[1]   Richard Murphy, "Syria's Foreign Policy: Looking Beyond the Gulf Crisis—The Prospects for Sustaining Improved Relations with the West," unpublished paper, June 1991, 3; see also Eisenstadt, *Arming for Peace*, 58.

[2]   *Foreign Report*, December 6, 1993.

[3]   Human Rights Watch, *World Report 1991*, 604.

decision or to resolve problems between them. Theodor Hanf describes this as the "satellization of Lebanon."

> In 1992 a Syro-Lebanese summit was held every forty days on average, and ministers and top civil servants made hundreds of trips to Damascus. Syria's leaders settle internal Lebanese disputes between the president, prime minister and speaker of the chamber of deputies. Parliamentary candidates prior to the election and deputies since then vie with each other for the patronage of various groups close to the centre of power in Syria. In Damascus the careers of Lebanese Army officers and civil servants are made or broken.[1]

Speaking candidly, President Ilyas al-Hirawi confessed of his shame that so many Lebanese travel to Damascus to discuss their differences: "We now disagree on the appointment of a doorman and go to Damascus to submit the problem to the brothers [there]."[2] Lebanese officials openly acknowledge that Damascus makes all the decisions in the peace process with Israel. The information minister says his government "will not sign any peace accord with Israel before there is a solution on the Syrian track. Our fate is linked to that of Syria."[3] In all, as Israeli military intelligence puts it, "Lebanon's dependence on Syria is absolute."[4]

The consequences for Lebanon of Syrian control are many. Before the Syrian intervention, Lebanon had been much the most open of the Arabic-speaking countries, boasting decentralized power, real democracy, unimpeded movement, a Hong Kong-style free market, independent schools, and an unfettered press. Now, the central government in Beirut keeps gaining in authority while—at least partly because of a Christian boycott of parliamentary elections—today's parliament might be "the least representative in Lebanese history."[5] The Syrian police control who comes into the country and who goes out. Assad's regime imposes Syrian-style standards on the school curricula, including the requirement that Arabic and Islam be taught. It brings the free-wheeling Lebanese economy more in line with that of statist Syria, creates organic links between the two countries (for example, in the electricity grid and in roads), and dumps Syrian goods in Lebanon.

As for the press, long the freest in the Arabic-speaking countries, Human Rights Watch states that it "has been forced to toe a Syrian-drawn line, leave Syrian-controlled Lebanon, or cease functioning."[6] At

---

[1] Theodor Hanf, *Coexistence in Wartime Lebanon: Decline of a State and Rise of a Nation,* translated from German by John Richardson (London: I.B. Tauris, 1993), 642.

[2] *Al-Diyar* (Beirut), December 3, 1994.

[3] *Al-Yawm* (Dammam), August 7, 1994.

[4] Uri Saguy, then-head of Israeli military intelligence, *Davar,* September 5, 1994.

[5] Hanf, *Coexistence in Wartime Lebanon,* 632.

[6] Human Rights Watch, *World Report 1991,* 605.

one point, on March 23, 1994, the government suddenly prohibited all private television stations from broadcasting news—or even speeches by the prime minister. In the best Syrian style of mumbo-jumbo, the Lebanese information minister explained: "Our objective behind this measure is to ensure a stronger commitment by everyone to the law and to the ongoing efforts to boost the national decision and services."[1] Translation: some news broadcasts were too friendly to Israel. Also, the Lebanese-Syrian security agreement of September 1991 provides for a mutual ban on activities that would harm the other country, including hostile media coverage. Accordingly, the government has strictly forbidden the press from criticizing Syrian leaders or Syrian policy.

These steps have the additional virtue, from Assad's point of view, of making life in Lebanon less attractive to the Christian population there, and especially to the Maronites who are the heart of independent Lebanon. Lebanese Christians already have a century's legacy of emigration and the Syrianization of their country makes it likely they will abandon their ancestral home in ever-increasing numbers. Should they do so, Damascus will have cleared Lebanon from the major obstacle to its permanent colonization of that country.

Palestinians. Assad and Arafat have competed for decades and famously despise each other. As early as 1966, Assad arrested Arafat and jailed him for more than a month. Since then, Damascus has often tried to undercut the PLO. Their forces battled in Lebanon from 1976 to 1983, when Syrian troops finally defeated PLO fighters and compelled Arafat to beat an ignominious retreat. Two years later, Assad cobbled the various Palestinian groups based in Damascus into the Palestine National Salvation Front to replace the PLO as the premier Palestinian organization. Assad then systematically exploited diplomatic opportunities to undermine PLO claims to leadership.

Arafat responded in kind. Calling the Syrian leadership "Zionists who speak Arabic,"[2] he lambasted its effort to take over the Palestinian nationalist movement. In PLO eyes, Assad's actions against the Palestinians meant he had "plunged into the morass of apostasy and treason."[3] Arafat did not deign to acknowledge the existence of the Damascus-based Palestinian organizations. When pressed, he referred to the Palestine National Salvation Front as "a front that bombed Palestinian camps [in Lebanon]."[4]

Against this backdrop of hostility, it comes as something of a surprise to learn that Assad and Arafat have had extensive contacts, nearly all cordial, since the end of the Kuwait War. Within days of the signing of the Syrian-Lebanese Treaty of Brotherhood, Cooperation,

---

[1] Michel Samaha, Radio Lebanon, March 25, 1994.

[2] Iraqi News Agency, July 14, 1988.

[3] *Al-Sha'b* (Jerusalem), July 11, 1988.

[4] *Filistin al-Muslima*, August 1, 1991.

and Coordination in May 1991, Assad released 1,500 Palestinian detainees and gave up his attempts to topple Arafat as the PLO's leader. PLO media not only spoke of an "atmosphere of concord and agreement," but offered it as an example for other Arab leaders to emulate.[1] When Arafat visited Damascus in October 1991, Assad received him with all the honor due a chief of state.

Assad vilified the signing of the Israel-PLO Declaration of Principles as a sellout of the Palestinian cause, yet he did not engage in an all-out effort to block it. He claimed to see the DOP as an inconsequential step, not worthy of his notice. "I did not consider it a significant event. Nor do I think it will have great effect."[2] Why not? Because it will probably fail. "We have not obstructed them [the PLO leaders]. Thus far, we feel their political moves have not posed a real threat. We do not think they will lead to the happy ending expected by some people. In any case, we are watching, and we will wait and see."[3] If, by chance, the Declaration of Principles does not fail, Assad says he can scuttle it. "Had we wanted to obstruct it, we would have foiled it. If it becomes clear to us that its harm is great, we will do so."[4] Here, he signals his determination, as ever, to dominate Palestinian decisionmaking if it moves in directions he disapproves of.

Even after the DOP was signed, Arafat traveled to Qardaha, the Assad home town, to offer his condolences on the death of Basil al-Assad. There, Arafat spoke of "the longstanding, strong relationship [with Hafez al-Assad as] . . . a brotherly relation between us that developed thirty years ago."[5] Of course, none of this rhetoric should be taken at face value; the rivalry continues, but in a more subtle way.

Jordan. When it comes to Jordan, the peace process dominates Syrian concerns; Assad does not like King Hussein's bilateral peace treaty with Israel and views it as a threat to his claim to control the pace and direction of Arab action in the peace process. In a thinly veiled statement, Foreign Minister Sharaa warned Jordan in late 1993 that unilateral steps would have "negative repercussions on its internal situation and on its stability."[6] Indeed, since the mid-1980s, the king usually took his lead on Arab-Israeli matters from Damascus. Not only did Israelis recognize this constraint (a cabinet member in the Rabin government once called Assad "the only reason for the lack of progress in Israeli-Jordanian relations")[7] but the Jordanian prime minister publicly stated that his government would not sign a peace accord with

---

[1] Sawt Filastin (Algiers), May 29, 1991.

[2] Syrian Arab Television, October 2, 1993.

[3] *Al-Qabas*, December 9, 1989.

[4] *Al-Akhbar*, September 20, 1993.

[5] *Al-Wasat* (London), February 14-20, 1994.

[6] *Al-Diyar* (Beirut), October 27, 1993.

[7] Moshe Shahal, *Ha'aretz*, November 28, 1983.

Israel before Damascus did so.[1] Amman's willingness to follow Damascus's lead in lesser matters—such as going to signing ceremonies when Syrian diplomats do (Rabin and Arafat at the White House), staying away when they do not (Rabin and Arafat in Cairo)—confirmed this impression.

But in the end, Amman defied Damascus and signed a formal peace with Israel in October 1994, with President Clinton and thousands of other witnesses in attendance. A number of reasons explain the Jordanian move—concern about an emerging Israeli-PLO relationship, fear that Damascus would reach its own deal with Israel first, interest in economic benefits of peace, including debt relief. Damascus communicated its displeasure in a number of ways. Assad accused King Hussein of "apostasy" for agreeing to permit Israeli farmers land-use rights in territory ceded to Jordan; Syrian officials met leaders of radical Jordanian groups committed to the overthrow of the Hashemite regime; and a significant increase in infiltration across the Jordanian-Syrian frontier by Palestinian and other terrorists took place after the treaty signing.

Assad did not, however, make a concerted effort to sabotage Israel-Jordan relations, as he had done a decade earlier. "You have made a big mistake, but we will not make a fuss or fight you on this issue," he told the Jordanians.[2] It is unclear whether this relative docility on Assad's part reflects restraint on his part or an inability to bully the Jordanians as of old.

Iraq. From the moment Saddam Hussein invaded Kuwait in August 1990, Assad inveighed against this act on the grounds that it deprived the Arabs of a major source of strength to deploy against Israel. All along, he argued that the Arab states need to "restore" Iraq to the Arab body politic in order to regain this arsenal.[3] Toward this end, in 1991-92 he improved relations with the regime in Baghdad through gestures symbolic (posting Iraqi weather information on the television weather forecasts and reestablishing postal relations between the two countries) and substantial. The latter included calling off the media invective, letting contraband goods enter Iraq through Syrian territory, having his officials meet their Iraqi counterparts, weighing in against further UN military action against Iraq, and dropping hints about reopening the Iraqi pipeline to the Mediterranean Sea.

But, apparently dissatisfied with Baghdad's response, Assad subsequently adopted a tougher line toward his neighbor, closing down official contacts (with just two exceptions: engineers dealing with the Euphrates River water and minor officials dealing with border

---

[1] 'Abd al-Salam al-Majali, on Radio Jordan, November 8, 1993.

[2] Syrian Arab News Agency, October 18, 1994.

[3] *Al-Safir,* January 4, 1995.

problems).[1] Relations plummeted in early 1995, when the Syrians apparently concluded that Saddam Hussein's fall was imminent. In preparation, they took initiatives to make the Iraqi president's life more difficult by taking such steps as building a high sand barrier to prevent smuggling into Iraq—something vital for Saddam's survival. More important, they prepared for the coming strife.

Toward this end, Assad immersed himself in internal Iraqi affairs. A four-member Syrian team traveled to northern Iraq to "study conditions" there and to "coordinate" with the opposition leaders.[2] Perhaps not coincidentally, within a few months prominent anti-Saddam activists moved to Damascus (including two former generals and the brother of a third) and others visited for long periods. Opposition figures got to meet with regime leaders; one of them, Muhammad Baqir al-Hakim, had an audience with Assad himself and came away saying that Assad "shares our views on important matters."[3] An exiled Iraqi Ba'thist called for the overthrow of Saddam Hussein, while Vice President 'Abd al-Halim Khaddam denounced Saddam Hussein to foreign delegations, called on the Iraqi opposition groups to unite, and offered Syria's good offices to help them do so.[4] With luck, these mediating efforts would finish off the American-backed Iraqi National Congress and replace it with a Syrian-oriented organization.

The Syrian capital became the center of anti-Saddam intrigue and rhetoric. When fighting erupted in western Iraq between the Dulaym tribal confederation and the regime in June 1995, reinforcements of men and arms reportedly came from Syria.[5] Exile groups in Damascus (including the Supreme Assembly of the Islamic Revolution in Iraq, SAIRI, Iran's main anti-Saddam vehicle) publicly commemorated the deaths of those who fell at the authorities' hands. The defection of Saddam Hussein's two daughters and their powerful husbands to Jordan in August 1995 prompted gloating commentary in the Syrian press about the "start of the downfall" of the Iraqi regime.[6] Even though Assad later downplayed the importance of this defection, to Baghdad's intense relief, his government activism in 1995 has established it as one of the most significant powers in the shaping of a post-Saddam Iraq.

---

[1] Iraqi Foreign Minister Muhammad Sa'id al-Sahhaf, *al-Quds al-'Arabi*, February 16, 1995.

[2] *Al-Sharq al-Awsat*, March 8, 1995; see also *Al-Hayat*, March 11, 1995.

[3] Voice of Rebellious Iraq, August 6, 1995.

[4] Mahdi al-'Ubaydi, Kuwaiti News Agency, July 11, 1995; see also Khaddam on Syrian Arab Republic Radio, June 22, 1995; Radio Monte Carlo, July 23, 1995; and Voice of Rebellious Iraq, July 26, 1995.

[5] Agence France Presse, June 3, 1995. It bears noting that the Dulaym tribe extends into Syrian territory.

[6] *Al-Thawra*, August 12, 1995.

V CONFRONTATION WITH TURKEY

There is a hostile feeling from the Turkish people not against the Syrian people but against the regime in Syria, and I believe that Hafez al-Assad should be careful.

—Turgut Özal, president of Turkey[1]

Relations with Turkey may well be the worst Syria has with any state. The two sides differ on a wide range of issues, violence frequently flares up between them, and matters appear to be getting worse. Years of dispute and the absence of a negotiating process imbue their problems with an explosive potential.

Yet it is easy to overlook Syrian-Turkish tensions, and Westerners generally do. Damascus and Ankara do not engage in loud polemics but on the formal level maintain surprisingly cordial relations. Violent acts on Syria's part have usually been small-scale, away from the cities, and carried out by proxies. In Western bureaucracies, those responsible for Turkey tend to see it as a far region of NATO, while those concerned with Syria devote their attention mainly to the Arab-Israeli conflict. The bureaucratic difficulty is acute in the U.S. government, where Turkey lies within the jurisdiction of the European bureau and Syria in the Near East bureau; accordingly, Syrian-Turkish difficulties fall between two administrative stools.

Contentious Issues

Syria and Turkey differ over a wide range of issues. The Assad regime has three main grudges against the Republic of Turkey: it claims the Turkish province of Hatay, it wants to prevent Turks from controlling Euphrates River waters, and it fears Turkish membership in the Western alliance. For their part, Turks worry about Syrian smuggling and (most importantly) Syrian support of terrorist groups.

---

[1] *Al-Hayat,* December 15, 1991.

Hatay and beyond. Damascus lays claim to the Turkish province of Hatay (formerly known as Alexandretta; in Turkish, Iskenderun), a region that became Turkish in 1939 when the French (who controlled Syria at that time) made a deal with Ankara on the eve of World War II. No Syrian government has accepted that agreement and, every evening, the weather map on Syrian television shows Hatay as part of Syria. With similar regularity, Syria's United Nations delegation each year demands Hatay's return. The Syrians also have occasionally articulated aspirations to a territory about the size of England that lies south of the Taurus and Anti-Taurus Mountains. These territories became part of the Turkish republic in 1921, again as a result of a Franco-Turkish agreement.

These hints aside, Damascus avoids pressing a public claim to Turkish territory. A Turkish television interviewer put it straight to Foreign Minister Faruq al-Sharaa in mid-1992: "On the one hand, you talk about Turkey's territorial integrity and good-neighborly relations and on the other your maps show Antakya and Iskenderun as Syrian territory. Don't you think that there is a contradiction here?" Sharaa avoided giving much of an answer, neither asserting a Syrian claim nor denying it:

> I believe that such misunderstandings between our countries will be resolved through political and economic cooperation and the atmosphere of mutual trust we are trying to build. It is necessary to establish lasting cooperation between the two countries. I believe that we can thus solve all the problems that exist between Turkey and Syria.[1]

Though theoretical and distant, Syrian claims to Turkey's territory underlie many of the tensions between the two countries, and specifically the Syrian campaign of terrorism. Ali Oncu, a Turkish journalist, summed up a widespread Turkish suspicion: the Syrians support anti-Turkish activities "to fragment Turkey so they can annex Hatay."[2]

Euphrates River waters. When the Atatürk Dam, the fifth-largest dam in the world and the capstone of Turkey's giant Southeast Anatolia Development Project (GAP), began filling in November 1989, the Turkish government gained the ability to control how much of the Euphrates River waters would flow into Syria (and beyond it to Iraq). That river had carried about 850 cubic meters of water to Syria each second; in July 1987, Ankara had committed to provide at least 500 cubic meters of water a second. On balance, it has fulfilled this obligation (that is to say, it makes up for any instances of dipping under the 500 cubic meters a second). Still, the Syrian government blames many of its electricity and agricultural problems on the Turkish

---

[1]   Show Television (Ankara), August 17, 1992.
[2]   *Tercuman*, October 24, 1991.

dams. The dams constitute a new lever of power for Turkey with major political implications. Simply put, Ankara can now threaten to withhold water from Syria, a prospect that Turkish politicians have been known to relish in public. (Prime Minister Süleyman Demirel was quoted in 1992 as saying that "The water is ours on this side of the border and theirs on the other side.")[1] In times of relative drought especially (such as that which afflicted the region in mid-1989), this gives the Turks extraordinary clout. Second, because many Turks fail to understand the logic wherein they pay for Arab oil, but Arabs pay nothing for "Turkish water," the day may come when they demand some form of payment for the water Syria receives.[2] Third, the Syrians have directed some small-scale sabotage efforts against the dams (circumstantial evidence suggests that the eleven PKK members captured in December 1988 infiltrating from Syria intended to attack the Atatürk Dam); some day, the Syrians could conceivably deploy military force against the waterworks.

Turkey as a Western ally. As a member of the North Atlantic Treaty Organization (NATO), Turkey is a formal ally of the United States. With Syria firmly in the Soviet camp until 1991, this placed the two states on opposite sides of the great divide. Even today, when Damascus seeks improved relations with the West, Turkey's American connection rankles. Statements by Syrian leaders point to their suspicion that Ankara (like Jerusalem) takes orders from Washington.

The prospect of Turkish-Israeli cooperation evidently scares the Syrians greatly, and with good reason. Not only do the two states share important attributes as the two full democracies of the Middle East, but they also have similar problems with Syrian bellicosity. And as Turks become less reluctant to deal with Israel, the prospects of their cooperating *vis-à-vis* Syria increase.

Smuggling. Turning to Turkish problems with Syria, Turks intensely resent that their country has become an important transit route for drug trafficking between the Bekaa Valley and Europe. They see the Syrian *mukhabarat* overseeing the production of hashish and Indian

---

[1] *Turkish Times,* September 1, 1994. The Turkish government quickly backtracked, and recommitted to its obligations. For a detailed and reliable overview of the Syrian-Turkish water problem, see John F. Kolars and William A. Mitchell, *The Euphrates River and the Southeast Anatolia Development Project* (Carbondale, IL: Southern Illinois University Press, 1991).

[2] There is a good legal response to this argument, but the Syrian leadership has not articulated it. Foreign Minister Faruq al-Sharaa commented on the subject: "Although the source of a river may be in a given country, its waters may flow through several countries. The question of oil is different. Oil is extracted in several countries. The extracted oil remains in those countries" (*Milliyet,* August 14, 1992). Curiously, the Syrians make precisely the Turks' argument in the Israeli context; there, Vice President 'Abd al-Halim Khaddam announced, "water which springs from Syrian land is Syrian water" (*Financial Times* and *al-Sharq al-Awsat,* June 23, 1995). Damascus must make up its mind.

hemp, its processing into heroin, and transport to Western Europe.[1] To a lesser degree, agricultural contraband across the 800-kilometer long border also causes problems, as Syrians smuggle out agricultural goods to escape Syria's high tariffs and reach the Turkish markets where they can gain a better price. In past years, before Turkish border security was improved, as much value in cattle and expensive foodstuffs may have been smuggled across the border as was sent legally.

Terrorism

Terrorism became a major part of the Soviet-Syrian campaign against Turkey in the 1970s and is today the most important item on the Turkish agenda pertaining to Syria. Damascus has relied occasionally on leftist Turks to prosecute its campaign of intimidation against Turkey. But far more often it has turned to other ethnic groups—Palestinians, Greeks and Greek Cypriots, Armenians, and Kurds—to do its work.

Palestinians. In return for Assad's help, anti-Arafat Palestinian groups have on occasion served on Syria's behalf against Turkey. For example, Abu Nidal's organization took part in the massacre at Istanbul's Neve Shalom synagogue in September 1986. Since the mid-1980s, the Palestinian role, however, has been mostly indirect: not so much carrying out operations against Turks as training others who do; and (most helpfully) bringing the latter into contact with Damascus. George Habash's Popular Front for the Liberation of Palestine trained the Turkish group Dev-Sol and the Armenian ASALA in Lebanon and provided them with weapons; in return, members of these groups fought with the Palestinians, especially in 1982.[2] Other Palestinian groups made contact with the PKK in 1979 and helped to transform a motley band of irredentists into a significant force.

Greeks and Greek Cypriots. Perhaps to compensate for the loss of Soviet bloc backing, Assad has in recent years orchestrated a working alliance with Greeks and Armenians, two parties famously antagonistic to Turkey. In the former case, he provides enthusiastic support for the cause of (Christian) Greek Cypriots in their conflict with (Muslim) Turkish Cypriots; and he arranged for the Cyprus issue to be removed from the agenda of the Organization of the Islamic Conference, an unfriendly forum. Assad has some murky ties with Prime Minister Andreas Papandreou (for example, via the reputed Nicaraguan arms merchant, George Hallaq) and the PKK has such strong connections to Greece and Greek Cyprus that, according to a German report, it maintains several training camps in those two countries and Öcalan is in contact with their leaderships. (Panayiotis Sgouridhis, deputy

---

[1]   *Yeni Gunaydïn,* July 23, 1995.

[2]   *Milliyet,* August 21, 1982. For a specific example of this bond, see Raphael Israeli, *The PLO in Lebanon: Selected Documents* (New York: St Martin's Press, 1983), 191, 203.

speaker of the Greek parliament, publicly visited Öcalan in the Bekaa Valley). Turkish intelligence sources trace a large flow of PKK-sponsored drugs moving from their origins in Syrian-controlled territory through Greek Cyprus and Greece to their destination in Western Europe. Most revealing of all, captured PKK members have confessed that a Syrian national trained them in Greece on the production of explosives.[1]

It was not until June 1995, however, that the Greek-Syrian relationship became an open alliance; in that month, the two states signed a military cooperation agreement that included the exchange of information, Greek sales of equipment to Syria, common military exercises, and Syrian training methods taught to Greek officers. Turkish sources also reported that the agreement entails Greek use of Syrian air fields and even the possibility of a Greek base in Syria (for use against Turkish forces in Cyprus), but these met with denials.

Turks responded to the Greek-Syrian agreement with alarm, raising the specter of an "Athens-Nicosia-Damascus triangle . . . providing every assistance to the PKK" and seeing it as having "only one target and that is Turkey."[2] More dramatically, another politician[3] described Turkey as being "encircled by the PKK-Russia, PKK-Armenia, PKK-Syria, and now PKK-Athens." Athens had become so partisan that Syria's Prime Minister Mahmud al-Zu'bi deemed it the state most friendly to his country, following only the Arab states; in contrast, the Turkish military found Greece the country most engaged in promoting "everything that is anti-Turkish."[4] For all these reasons, President Demirel warned that "Greece must be very careful. It must avoid any activity that might upset Turkey."[5]

Armenians. Armenian nationalism arose in the 1860s with the goal of creating an independent Armenian state out of the then-decrepit Ottoman Empire; the failure of this goal and the mass killings of Armenians in 1915 created deep tensions between Armenians and Turks that yet endure. In about 1970, many Armenians, "in their search for a model," watched with admiration the way Palestinians succeeded in winning publicity for their cause.[6] Some Armenians joined the PLO, more or less as apprentices. According to one report, the Armenian Secret Army for the Liberation of Armenia (ASALA) was conceptualized in 1973 by Yasser Arafat's deputy, Salah Khalaf (also

---

[1] *Die Welt* (Berlin), December 2, 1994.

[2] *Yeni Gunaydïn,* July 23, 1995. See also former prime minister Mesut Yılmaz on TRT Television June 27, 1995. *Cumhuriyet,* June 22, 1995 notes efforts "to surround Turkey from the north, south, and west."

[3] True Path Party Deputy Whip Turhan Tayan, TRT Television, June 29, 1995.

[4] *I Kathimerini* (Athens), June 20, 1995; see also *Turkish Daily News,* July 3, 1995.

[5] *Milliyet,* July 3, 1995.

[6] Francis P. Hyland, *Armenian Terrorism: The Past, the Present, the Prospects* (Boulder, CO: Westview, 1991), 25.

known as Abu Iyad), and one of Khalaf's Armenian aides.[1] Starting in 1975, ASALA began a terrorist campaign against Turks and Westerners. The two organizations retained strong ties for some years: for example, when the PLO evacuated Beirut in August 1982, it apparently handed over many of its weapons to ASALA.

The liaison between ASALA and the PLO in due course led to a Syrian interest in ASALA, and the two developed close working relations. ASALA operatives made frequent use of Syrian territory; in particular, the ASALA agent who shot up the airport in Ankara on August 7, 1982, killing ten and injuring seventy-one, traveled this way. When ASALA split after the PLO left Lebanon, the more radical and violent elements reconstituted their headquarters in Damascus in 1983-84 and rebuilt their bases in the Bekaa Valley. ASALA later moved its training camp from there to locations in Syria (including one on the Turkish border at Qamishli). According to a historian of the Armenian terrorist movement, "ASALA received training, arms, and forged documents from Syria, accepting in return Syrian participation in the planning of ASALA attacks."[2] ASALA lost importance in the later 1980s.

Following which, the emergence in 1992 of an independent Armenia opened another front in the Syrian-Turkish confrontation. That President Levon Ter-Petrossian was the son of a Communist Party leader in Syria helped spur the connection, but a shared hostility to the Republic of Turkey provided the real basis of cooperation. Yerevan opened an embassy in Damascus in April 1993, during the depths of its war with Azerbaijan, and another in Beirut a year later. In turn, Assad promised 7,000 tons of fuel oil gratis to the Armenians. Azerbaijan's President Ebülfez Ali Elçibey announced in early 1993 that five hundred terrorists had arrived in Armenia from Lebanon, while his ambassador in Ankara asserted that Syrian citizens fought with Armenia against Azerbaijan.[3] Later that year, reports surfaced of PKK bases in Armenia.

Kurds. The world's roughly 20 million Kurds live mainly in four countries (Syria, Turkey, Iraq, Iran), with the largest numbers (over ten million) in Turkey. From the establishment of the Turkish republic in 1923, Kurds have engaged in a sporadic insurrection against the central government. In 1974 the Soviets sponsored a Marxist-Leninist organization of Turkish Kurds aiming to establish a separate Kurdish state in eastern Turkey that would be sympathetic to the USSR. The Worker's Party of Kurdistan (PKK), led by Abdullah Öcalan (known as Apo) took an active part in the spiral of violence and terror that enveloped Turkey in the late 1970s; by the early 1980s, it had become the single greatest menace to Turkish domestic security. Today, after

---

[1]   Ibid., 57.

[2]   Ibid., 49.

[3]   Interfax, April 15, 1993; see also *Türkiye*, February 22, 1993.

10,000 and more deaths, the PKK controls substantial parts of eastern Turkey, especially at night.

Since 1979, the organization has relied heavily on Syrian help. In that year, Öcalan approached Palestinians in Syria for aid, training, and connections, all of which they supplied. By 1980, Öcalan had become a client of the Syrian regime, and of Hafez al-Assad's two brothers, Jamil and Rif'at, in particular. The Syrians provided him with a three-story residence (in a district of Damascus normally off-limits to foreigners), an armored Mercedes, and a bodyguard contingent of Syrian Kurds. "In every way," Ismet G. Imset observes, "he was living the life of a Syrian official."[1] PKK troops were outfitted, trained, and deployed by the Syrian army; indeed, ethnic Kurds who are Syrian nationals joined the PKK in increasing numbers and with ever greater responsibilities. In October 1993, official Turkish sources claimed that "Syrian commanders are leading some PKK terror units."[2] Estimates put the number of Syrians involved in the fighting at 300-500. In short, the PKK became a subsidiary of the Syrian state, receiving from it, among other benefits, places to live, money, weapons, ammunition, and false passports. In addition, the PKK used Syrian facilities to meet the foreign press and stage party congresses.[3]

In 1982, the PKK proved its mettle by fighting Israeli forces in Lebanon but lost its Lebanese training camps as a result of the Israeli occupation. The Syrian authorities rewarded it with permission to train on Syrian territory and with a large camp in the Bekaa Valley, which became its headquarters. According to one scholar, by 1984, "the PKK had lost most of its operational freedom, having found it necessary to clear most of its operations first with the Syrian *mukhabarat* [intelligence services]."[4] That same year, the PKK began using Syria as a base to launch cross-border raids into Turkey. In 1991, Öcalan claimed to have "hundreds of camps" in Lebanon; while clearly an exaggeration, a reporter did witness that Palestinians and Turks used PKK facilities.[5]

The PKK has established its main political office in Germany, where it actively propagandizes and recruits among the Turks resident

---

[1]   Ismet G. Imset, *The PKK: A Report on Separatist Violence in Turkey 1973-1992* (Ankara: Turkish Daily News, 1992), 32.

[2]   State of Emergency Governor Ünal Erkan, *Sabah*, November 2, 1993.

[3]   Imset, *The PKK*, 171-72.

[4]   Suha Bolukbasi, "Ankara, Damascus, Baghdad, and the Regionalization of Turkey's Kurdish Secessionism," *Journal of South Asian and Middle Eastern Studies*, (Summer 1991): 18.

[5]   *Turkish Daily News*, November 28, 1991; see also *Jerusalem Report*, March 19, 1992. Asked about a huge crashing sound at a PKK camp, a guard pointed to two buildings on a nearby hill and told the reporter, "It's only the Palestinians. We gave them the place and they're training. They're good people but all graduates die," (*Turkish Daily News*, December 4, 1991).

in that country. In addition, the organization maintains nearly a hundred branches throughout Western Europe. Syrian embassies maintain close contact with the PKK in places as diverse as Stockholm and Madrid, providing useful services and receiving various forms of help in return.[1] Although some Western states officially acknowledge the PKK's record of terror,[2] the organization continues to enjoy a legal status in several European countries and recently established a parliament-in-exile in Holland.

Clashing over the PKK

While many issues rile Turkish-Syrian relations, two have emerged as paramount: Turkish control of Euphrates waters and Syrian sponsorship of the PKK. In Syrian eyes, these two issues are closely intertwined, as Assad has, over the years, either used or withdrawn his trump card (Kurds) against the Turkish trump (water). Syrian officials sometimes make this connection explicit: "If we can reach an agreement on the important issue of water, our people will view Turkey with more affinity and sympathy."[3] In Turkish eyes, however, the two issues cannot be connected. Water is a conventional diplomatic issue to be bargained over, like many others (coastal shelves, fishing rights); terrorism is another story altogether. As Ankara sees it, to reward Assad for sponsoring the PKK would encourage him to use this instrument to raise other questions, such as Turkish control of Hatay province.

Until 1987, Syrian authorities categorically denied Öcalan's presence in their country or any state support for the PKK. Only when the Turks made clear how much they knew (including the address of Öcalan's domicile in Damascus) did the Syrians acknowledge his presence. Then the real diplomatic jousting began. In July 1987, the two governments signed a Security Protocol, during a state visit by then-Prime Minister Turgut Özal to Damascus, in which they promised to "obstruct groups engaged in destructive activities directed against one another on their own territory and would not turn a blind eye to them in any way."[4] Instead, the Syrian authorities moved Öcalan to new residences and relocated most PKK facilities from Lebanon (where Turkish forces might attack them, Israeli-style) to Syria (where they were much safer). During Özal's second visit in August 1988, the Syrians reiterated their earlier promise, but nothing changed. In fact, the situation worsened to the point that Özal took the unprecedented step on October 1, 1989 of publicly threatening Damascus that if it

---

[1]   Anat Kurz and Ariel Merari, *ASALA: Irrational Terror or Political Tool?* (Boulder, CO: Westview, 1985), 44.

[2]   See, for example, Department of State, *Patterns of Global Terrorism, 1994* (Washington, DC: Department of State Publication, 1995), 47.

[3]   Foreign Minister Faruq al-Sharaa, Show Television (Ankara), June 16, 1995.

[4]   *Milliyet,* July 18, 1987, quoted in *Middle East Contemporary Survey,* vol. 11, 675.

failed to live up to the 1987 Security Protocol, Ankara would turn off the water flowing across the border, and he added, "We are doubtful they are abiding by these conditions."[1] This warning led to a reduction in PKK attacks, but not for long. A pattern evolved over the next years: Turkish threats, a lull, a new round of attacks; then Turkish threats and the cycle repeats itself.

In early 1992, Ankara became so disturbed by PKK assaults, Foreign Minister Hikmet Çetin announced that "Turkey's relations with Syria will henceforth be affected by the line that country takes on the question of PKK terrorism."[2] In other words, it effectively reduced the bilateral relationship with Damascus to a test of PKK behavior; and for the first time, Turkish officials began speaking publicly about the PKK problem. When asked about the PKK presence, Syrian officials had difficulty providing a satisfactory answer. Bushra Kanafani of the Syrian embassy in Washington replied that her government has "a moral commitment to people who have been there [Damascus] a long time; we can't just throw them out."[3]

In April 1992, Turkey's Interior Minister Ismet Sezgin traveled to Damascus with four bulging files establishing Syrian backing for the PKK and demanded a cessation of support for the PKK. The Syrians got the message; indeed, Sezgin reported they were so accommodating that during his four-hour meeting with Assad, the Syrian leader held Sezgin's hand for fifteen minutes![4] Sezgin came away with a second Security Protocol which, in his understanding, meant the Syrians agreed to declare that "the PKK [is] a terrorist organization illegal in Syria, that they will constantly monitor the activities in Syria of organizations that perpetuate terrorist activities against Turkey, and that they will arrest and try the members of that murderous gang when apprehended."[5] Further, his Syrian counterpart made soothing noises ("Whatever disturbs Turkey disturbs us as well") and promised "nice surprises."[6] To all this, Turkey's Defense Minister replied ominously, "there will be no need to bomb Bekaa if Syria is sincere in what it said about the PKK."[7]

News soon came from Syria and Lebanon of Öcalan decamping and the bases shutting down. A top PKK leader told the Associated Press, "I am here today with a few comrades to pick up some personal

---

[1] *Gunaydin*, October 2, 1989; see also *Financial Times*, October 23, 1989.

[2] *Hürriyet*, February 26, 1992.

[3] George Gruen, "Syria, Syrian Jews, and the Peace Process," unpublished paper, June 1992, 13.

[4] *Turkish Daily News*, April 23, 1992.

[5] Turkey's Interior Minister Ismet Sezgin, TRT Television, April 21, 1992.

[6] Syria's Interior Minister Muhammad Harba, *Turkish Daily News*, April 23, 1992; see also Foreign Minister Faruq al-Sharaa, Anatolia News Agency, June 17, 1992.

[7] Imset, *The PKK*, 178.

stuff."[1] Prime Minister Süleyman Demirel asserted that the PKK's headquarters in Syria "no longer exists."[2] The Turkish interior minister stated categorically that the PKK had "completely" left the Bekaa Valley and speculated that Öcalan had sought refuge in the chaos of northern Iraq.[3] Others subsequently located him in Beirut, in Greece, in the Greek part of Cyprus, or Armenia. Syria's foreign minister declared Syrian-Turkish relations "at their best level since World War II, if not since World War I."[4] This became the official line: as late as February 1993, the Turkish foreign minister asserted that "there are no activities in Syria that disturb Turkey."[5] And, indeed, PKK terrorism did temporarily halt.

But the Turkish military expressed skepticism, and with reason. By late July 1992, just three months after the second security protocol, reports came of Öcalan in the Bekaa Valley and the main PKK camp there in operation. In September 1992, angry noises began coming out of Ankara: "Syria will reap a storm."[6] In December, reports surfaced of a new PKK camp at some remove from the Bekaa Valley. In January 1993, a Turkish newspaper said Öcalan was being kept "in a very special location by Syria and is protected by intelligence agents;"[7] indeed, when pressed later that month by a Turkish interviewer about Öcalan's presence, Syria's Prime Minister Mahmud al-Zu'bi pointedly refused to reply. When the reporter insisted ("are you prepared to hand Abdullah Öcalan to Turkey if you arrest him?"), the prime minister simply replied, with a frown, "I prefer you not to ask me that question."[8] Also in early 1993, a PKK radio station began transmitting from Damascus at the unlikely frequency of 7.040 megahertz on the short-wave band. Syrian leaders acknowledged the PKK's presence but, as in the case of extremist Palestinian groups they host, maintained that it was prohibited from using force.

Matters continued to worsen as Turks got thoroughly fed up with Syrian mischief. Prime Minister Tansu Çiller's adviser on foreign affairs traveled to Damascus in early November 1993 and delivered what was said to be an unusually strong statement. Çetin publicly warned Assad: "Turkey cannot tolerate terrorist attacks from any of its neighbors. No one should think Turkey will remain silent about such attacks. The

---

[1] *Turkish Daily News* dispatch dated May 8, 1992, in *Turkish Times*, June 1, 1992.

[2] Hélène da Costa, "Entretien avec Suleyman Demirel," *Politique Internationale* (Summer 1992): 352.

[3] Ismet Sezgin, *Milliyet*, June 11, 1992. Two and a half years later (e.g., *Sabah*, December 2, 1994) Öcalan again was said to have moved to northern Iraq, though days later he was reportedly back in Syria (*Sabah*, December 16, 1994).

[4] Syrian Arab Republic Radio, August 1, 1992.

[5] Foreign Minister Hikmet Çetin, Anatolia News Agency, February 20, 1993.

[6] *Milliyet*, September 14, 1992.

[7] *Tercuman*, January 14, 1993.

[8] *Milliyet*, January 20, 1993.

necessary answer will be given." Çetin noted the Syrian denial but said it was "natural" for Ankara to have "difficulties in believing that."[1]

As ever, Damascus replied with the requisite words. On November 20, 1993, a Syrian major general from the Interior Ministry traveled to Ankara and signed an agreement promising that Syria would not serve as a "shelter" or a "passage" for anti-Turkish elements. He also assured the Turks that, if caught, Öcalan would be returned to Turkey.[2] Then, in a novel step, the Syrian state minister for foreign affairs, Nasir Qaddur, went on Turkish television and made what he called "a very important announcement": "The PKK has been declared illegal in Syria. The PKK is considered illegal in accordance with our laws. In brief, the PKK has been banned in Syria. . . . From now on, the PKK or Öcalan may not make use of or pass through Syrian territory."[3] In the aftermath of these iron-clad assurances, Turkish media reported that Öcalan had been arrested or expelled from Syria.

But, again, the issue did not die; already in January 1994, Interior Minister Mahit Menteşe publicly took issue with the Syrians' claim that Öcalan had left their country. In February, the Syrian foreign minister stonewalled his Turkish counterpart's protests about the PKK. Menteşe made the by-now familiar trek to Damascus in April 1994 to protest Öcalan and the PKK's continued presence in Syria and Lebanon. According to a purported record of his conversation with Syria's Interior Minister Muhammad Harba, Menteşe said he had evidence not only of Öcalan's presence in Syrian-controlled areas but proof that PKK rocket launchers captured in Turkey had come via Syria.[4] Menteşe again heard the right words from Harba but seven years of all talk and no action left him skeptical. "The Syrians," he said, "have responded positively to the problems presented by Turkey and its request for cooperation on those issues." But that was not enough: "We have to see concrete results."[5]

When Mümtaz Soysal replaced Hikmet Çetin as Turkey's foreign minister in July 1994, he reduced the pressure on Damascus (for example, he pointedly refused to request Öcalan's extradition). After a trip to Damascus, Soysal declared himself "less pessimistic" about relations with Syria because the Assad regime accepted his proposal that the two states begin with the easier issues (border crossing, land ownership, trade), then move on to the more challenging ones (the PKK and water). This, he hoped, would create "an atmosphere of mutual understanding." The tone of the bilateral relationship clearly did improve; for example, a Turkish firm won an unprecedented $30

---

[1] *Turkish Times*, December 1, 1993.

[2] Anatolia News Agency, November 20, 1993.

[3] Show Television (Ankara), December 6, 1993.

[4] *Hürriyet*, April 14, 1994.

[5] TRT Television, April 12, 1994.

million contract in Syria. In September 1994, the Syrian authorities canceled a press conference Öcalan had arranged in Lebanon. But before Soysal's efforts could have much lasting effect, he resigned his position in November 1994.

Relations resumed their tense quality. Soysal's successor, Murat Karayalcın, announced in his maiden speech as foreign minister that he could not say that Syrian support for anti-Turkish terrorist organizations had come to an end.[1] When asked by journalists on a plane ride about Syria, Prime Minister Çiller's "attractive face suddenly darkened" as she replied with uncharacteristic vehemence: "Turkey is a friend with its neighbors. But those who harbor enmity against us should fear our enmity. I am emphasizing this, let them fear our enmity."[2] Whether by design or accident, the Turkish authorities in May 1995 decreased the flow of water into Syria to just 200-300 cubic meters a second during the Feast of Sacrifice, the premier holiday of the Islamic calendar, explaining that maintenance work had to be done. Former prime minister Mesut Yılmaz declared Syria "increasingly hostile."[3]

Reflections

Syria, Turkey, and Israel. Though rarely looked at in tandem, Syrian disputes with Turkey and Israel share a number of features. Both revolve around territory once Syrian and still claimed by Damascus, Hatay (lost in 1939) and the Golan Heights (lost in 1967). In both cases, terrorism and water have central importance. Assad sponsors a dozen or so terrorist groups—ethnic, religious, ideological—against each of Turkey and Israel. New dams in Turkey permit Ankara to make life-and-death decisions about the quantity of Euphrates River water flowing into Syria; Syrian threats to divert the Jordan's tributaries could (were Damascus to recover the Golan Heights) deprive Israel of a substantial portion of its water supplies. Further, because Turkey and Israel are the two key allies of the United States in the Middle East, one a member of NATO and the other a partner in the most special of the United States's many special relationships, their problems with Syria take on a parallel international dimension as well.

Despite the intense attention to Syria's confrontation with Israel, a face-off with Turkey may present a more imminent danger. Consider these differences:

• The conflict with Israel is an old one, which Damascus long ago lost and militarily can have few expectations of winning in the future. In contrast, the conflict with Turkey is yet mounting, with new issues (such as water and the PKK) supplementing old ones (Hatay). Also, as

---

[1]   *Turkish Daily News*, December 19, 1994.

[2]   *Türkiye*, April 12, 1995.

[3]   TRT Television, June 27, 1995.

the conflict with Israel winds down, this could free up resources for use against Turkey, a possibility Ankara finds increasingly worrisome.

• The world closely follows the conflict with Israel, so for Damascus to choose war against Israel would be tantamount to renouncing its campaign to win Western favor. But the conflict with Turkey is obscure, so fighting presumably would not much affect Assad's standing in the West.

• The U.S. government would likely assist Israel in the case of war with Syria. Although Turkey is a NATO ally, American assistance against Damascus seems unreliable at best, in part because of German reluctance to have NATO help Turkey.

The Syrian claim to parts of Turkey represents one of the many back-burner, open-ended issues of the Middle East (like the Iraqi claim to Kuwait as its nineteenth province) that could unexpectedly flare up and create a serious crisis. This revanchist pretension is most likely to become active if the other contentious issues, terrorism and water, cannot be reconciled. Indeed, Murhaf Jouejati, a Syrian-American who has consulted for the government in Damascus, has publicly speculated that Turkey and Syria "are on a collision course" unless they can resolve their differences.[1]

Turkish impatience has potentially ominous implications for Damascus. Although Syrian military strength is considerable, it is heavily deployed in Lebanon and versus Israel, leaving little to spare for the north. Also, an American military analyst notes, Assad's forces "could not get tanks to the Turkish border except by driving them," which would be slow and would greatly damage the tracks and engines. (Of course, as the Turkish press points out,[2] peace with Israel would free up these forces and weapons.) In contrast, Turkish military forces are redeploying from the Aegean region to the southeast of Anatolia (mostly to deal with the PKK), where they will be conveniently located to deal with Syria. Some 40,000 soldiers are stationed near the border with Syria. Only slightly exaggerating, a former U.S. ambassador to Damascus observes that "the only thing that would delay the Turks in an invasion of Syria would be the need to stop and drink tea."

Controlled friction. Tensions along the Syria-Turkish border may be characterized as a limited Syrian irredentism toward Turkey deterred but not eliminated by Turkish counterpressures. Damascus seeks to annex parts of Turkish territory and render Ankara incapable of challenging its sway. If it cannot have what it wants—and it cannot just now—Damascus seeks to build strength while maintaining normal relations until new opportunities arise.

---

[1] Remarks at a United States Institute of Peace conference in Washington, DC, June 2, 1994.

[2] See, for example, *Cumhuriyet,* June 22, 1995.

In a typical example of Assad's ability to manage contradictory policies at once, Syrian-Turkish relations proceed along two tracks, one publicly correct and at times even friendly, the other privately hostile and suspicious. The two discourses remain for the most part separate, with foreign ministries handling the friendly portfolio and interior ministries the hostile one.[1]

A second double game plays out within the first. After a number of Syrian-backed terrorist incidents take place, followed by Syrian denials of guilt, a Turkish delegation goes to Damascus and presents the authorities there with hard evidence. The Syrians reject the evidence but at the same time assure the Turks that they will make sure the problem does not recur. They do for a while, and matters calm down. Then, some months later, Syrian backed terror against Turkey mounts again. A Turkish delegation takes off for Damascus, and the process begins over again.

War or peace ahead? There are reasons to expect Turkish-Syrian relations to remain calm, with many mutual visits, plenty of communications, and a shared interest in keeping up appearances. A series of small agreements (on the selling of electricity from Turkey to Syria and promoting tourism) point to a building of relations. The frontier area has become more relaxed; for example, in the 1980s, the Turkish and Syrian governments began to permit archaeologists and geologists from abroad—including the United States—to work near the border. The two sides have lived with each other in peace since Syrian independence, and both governments know that more is to be lost from fighting than gained by it. The two states actively cooperate *vis-à-vis* Iraq, with their foreign ministers meeting several times a year to discuss strategy. Common bonds forged by history and religion should temper future problems. Also, Turkey's leverage from its water projects may lead to a greater degree of Syrian caution.

The Greek card may provide another reason to expect quiet on the Turkish-Syrian border. In an unusually blunt series of articles, former Turkish ambassador to the United States Sükrü Elekdağ suggested that Ankara endure the indignities directed its way from Damascus out of fear of an "undisclosed alliance" against it between Syria and Greece:

> Turkey has decided that a heated clash with Syria will create a suitable situation for Greece to realize its objectives in the Aegean region. That will force Turkey to fight on two fronts. This assessment has prevented Turkey from adopting a determined policy against Syria.[2]

---

[1] Curiously, the more Turks protest Syrian transgressions, the more Assad's people lay on the politeness. Thus, the Syrian media used phrases like "friendly and positive" and "cordiality and friendship" to describe what must have been an intensely adversarial visit by Interior Minister Ismet Sezgin to Damascus in April 1992, when he secured a second Syrian agreement not to support the PKK.

[2] *Milliyet*, December 2-4, 1994.

Elekdağ points to the worrisome implications of a Syrian-Israeli peace: while a rough military balance now exists along the Turkish-Syrian boundary, a treaty with Israel would lead to a great strengthening of Syria's forces there; thus emboldened, Syrian support for the PKK would increase, thereby forcing more Turkish troops to deal with the internal front. He concludes that his government must plan to fight two and a half wars simultaneously—against Greece, Syria, and the PKK.

While Elekdağ calls for caution, years of abiding by Syrian transgressions leaves other Turks so frustrated and angry that they openly demand the use of coercive measures against Damascus. Proposals have aired in the Turkish press to block the Euphrates waters, adopt the "methods used by Israel" to destroy the PKK camps and kill Öcalan, strike at PKK camps in Lebanon, cut off the Euphrates waters, and wage "all-out war against Syria."[1]

The relative quiet of recent years reflects not an absence of problems but a Turkish determination to contain them. The Turkish position has gradually hardened as the leadership feels that Assad is trying to make fools of them; it may not be willing indefinitely to accept this treatment. Assad may be playing a double game with an opponent unwilling to go along with his subtle turns. The Turkish-Syrian border could unexpectedly and rapidly become a crisis point.

---

[1] Fatih Cekirge, *Sabah,* July 24, 1993; see also Evren Değer, *Cumhuriyet,* November 16, 1993; and Gungor Mengi, *Sabah,* November 7, 1993.

VI   NEGOTIATIONS WITH ISRAEL

Assad has made a strategic decision to opt for peace.

—Shimon Peres[1]

Israel and Syria share a strategic interest in attaining peace between them.

—Yitzhak Rabin[2]

I am not sure that Syria knows for a fact that there will be peace with us.

—Ehud Barak[3]

Syria's conflict with Israel began the day before the State of Israel was proclaimed; on May 14, 1948, Syrian artillery on the Golan Heights—a plateau of 425 square miles (1,100 square kilometers) with steep escarpments on several sides—assaulted Jewish settlements in the valley below. In June 1967, those same heights fell under Israeli control in the course of the Six Day War. A week later, on June 19, the Israeli government quietly offered to return Syrian territory on condition that Damascus agree to sign a peace treaty, establish demilitarized zones, and guarantee Israeli water sources.[4] Though flatly rejected at the time and rescinded by Jerusalem in October 1968, a version of this same offer appears to be, close to three decades later, back on the table.

Before 1991, Syria consistently had the toughest policy of Israel's neighbors, defined by five no's: no talks before a commitment to full withdrawal, no direct negotiations with Israel, no partial solutions, no separate deal for the Golan Heights, and no formal peace treaty. With only slight exceptions (such as the May 1974 Separation of Forces

---

[1] *Al Hamishmar,* March 25, 1994.

[2] Speech at the National Press Club, November 16, 1993. Rabin also noted with irony that Syrian support for groups attacking Israel "does not prove that Syria has made a strategic decision to make peace with Israel" (*al-Musawwar,* April 22, 1994).

[3] *Ha'aretz,* August 27, 1993.

[4] Abba Eban discusses this offer in *Jerusalem Post International Edition,* October 15, 1994.

Agreement), Assad kept consistently to these guidelines. Hardly an Israeli accepted these terms, however, and certainly neither of the two main political parties, so Syrian policy effectively foreclosed negotiations with Israel.

A major shift took place in the aftermath of the Kuwait War, when Assad accepted a joint Soviet-American invitation to join Arab-Israeli peace negotiations. Assad's July 1991 decision to send his foreign minister to the Madrid conference in October broke a strict, decades-old Syrian policy of refusing to meet officially with Israelis, and so amounted to something new and important. This move instantly negated two of the no's (no talks before a commitment to full withdrawal, no direct negotiations with Israel). Since the Madrid conference, Jerusalem and Damascus have maintained communication, either directly or through the Americans.

The negotiations fall into four distinct periods; Likud in office (October 1991 to June 1992), Labor taking over (July 1992 to August 1993), the Israel-PLO Declaration of Principles (September 1993 to March 1994), and the beginning of serious negotiations (April 1994 on). While the inside story of these talks remains officially unavailable, the public record is quite complete; or as Daniel Kurtzer, an American diplomat in the know, observes, "It is remarkable. . . how little is secret in the Syria-Israel negotiations."[1]

Negotiations did not flourish during Likud's tenure. For eight months, Syrian and Israeli diplomats both gave the impression they participated in the negotiations more to please the U.S. government than to conduct business. Specifically, Damascus made three demands of Israel: complete return of the Golan Heights, complete Israeli withdrawal from Lebanon, and the fulfillment of Palestinian national rights. Likud officials insisted on "peace for peace" (i.e., no return of the Golan Heights) and used the talks to affirm that the Syrians maintained their historic hostility to the Jewish state and that the Likud could still entice Arabs to the bargaining table, even with its uncompromising "not-one-inch" stance. In effect, Damascus and the Likud Party tacitly agreed to mark time.

"Withdrawal on the Golan Heights"

Optimism. The mood changed dramatically when Yitzhak Rabin and Shimon Peres came to office. Faced with an Israeli government willing to make concessions, Assad had to respond or he would look bad in American eyes. He did so in ways small (his negotiators now drank coffee with their Israeli counterparts) and large (presenting a working paper in August 1992 which even three years later remains the basis of discussions). A key difference in purpose quickly emerged: whereas Israelis saw the negotiations as a means to achieve peace with Syria,

---

[1] Policy Forum at The Washington Institute for Near East Policy, February 16, 1995.

Assad (as ever) saw them as a means to regain the lost Golan Heights and improve his standing in the West. What to Jerusalem was a "peace process" to Damascus was a "withdrawal process." This contrast created some complex dynamics.

Rabin's first major statement indicated he would countenance territorial compromise—i.e., withdrawal "on the Golan Heights," not "from" them.[1] To this, Assad responded with an offer of "the peace of the brave, the peace of the knights" with Israel.[2] Though welcome to Israeli ears, this formulation was not nearly specific enough. When Assad offered "full peace for full withdrawal,"[3] Jerusalem responded with cheers for this elaboration but again asked for more details: "although this [phrase] was positive, it was hardly useful."[4] What is the nature of "full peace"—what the United States has with Canada or with Cuba? Something in between? Does it refer to reaching an agreement with Israel only in the context of a comprehensive Arab-Israeli settlement? Jerusalem waited for Damascus to take the next step, but Assad declined.

An impasse resulted, occasioning near-insults. The Syrian media blamed it on Israeli unwillingness to make peace. In turn, Shimon Peres complained that "The Syrians are playing a game I do not like at all. They talk peace but they do not mean it."[5] The impasse grew worse as the Israelis dismissed the Syrian delegation to the talks as a "tape recorder" which plays back "a tune which never varies" and "constantly wants to be heard even if it does not listen."[6] They also called for elevating the talks to a higher political level and asked to make them private, away from the Washington media. The Syrians refused both requests. With arguments over so many issues and no resolution, the talks appeared deadlocked. By Israeli count, the two sides differed on at least fifty-two areas of substance.

---

[1] Rabin and his aides repeatedly drew attention to this distinction. See, for example, Kol Yisra'el, March 1, 1993.

[2] *Al-Thawra*, September 9, 1992. Steve Rodan ("Behind Closed Doors," *Jerusalem Post International Edition*, December 10, 1994) has credibly established that as early as October 1992, Rabin reached a private, non-binding understanding with the Syrians on the need for a full Israeli withdrawal from the Golan Heights. This then provided the basis for all the negotiations that followed. If true, all the public animosity appears to have been staged. Hussein Agha, a Lebanese scholar involved in some of the talks, points to the discrepancy: "Through third parties they [the Israelis] say yes [to full withdrawal]. Then publicly they say no."

[3] Patrick Seale, "'Full Peace for Full Withdrawal,'" *New York Times*, May 11, 1993. See also Seale's interview a day earlier in *al-Wasat*. Assad later slightly strengthened this formulation: "I understand that in return for a total withdrawal I will have to give total peace" (*Ha'aretz*, February 12, 1995).

[4] Itamar Rabinovich, "Smile When You Say Peace," *New York Times*, May 19, 1993.

[5] Israel Television, May 3, 1993.

[6] Shimon Peres, IDF Radio, May 5, 1993; see also Itamar Rabinovich, Israel Television, June 17, 1993.

Still, the two sides made some progress. While the Israelis complained about the paucity of confidence-building measures by Assad and he dismissed these as inappropriate ("I believe that in circumstances like ours, confidence-building measures are not the best way to resolve the problem under discussion"),[1] he did in fact offer some, including contacts with Israelis and reduced media hostility. More important yet, Assad implicitly stopped insisting on two more of his traditional no's. According to Clinton administration leaks, Secretary of State Warren Christopher found during his maiden voyage to Damascus in February 1993 that Assad offered to reach an agreement with Israel whose implementation would be phased in over time, in effect eliminating his traditional demand of immediate and full Israeli withdrawal.[2] Days later, Foreign Minister Sharaa dropped another long-standing rejection of a bilateral peace agreement outside the context of a unified, all-Arab accord with Israel: "although Syria is seeking a comprehensive arrangement, it also wants to conclude its negotiations with Israel as soon as possible and will therefore not necessarily wait for the conclusions of [Israel's] discussions with the Palestinians and other Arab countries."[3]

In July 1993, Hezbollah launched rockets from southern Lebanon against northern Israel, prompting massive retaliatory Israeli air bombings (Operation Accountability). Prior to 1991, this sequence of events could well have sparked a Syrian-Israeli confrontation. This time, Christopher brokered an understanding between Assad and Rabin in which Assad agreed to prevent Hezbollah—or anyone else—from launching Katyushas into the Galilee. Assad gained from the incident by getting more direct control over some dangerous allies, extending his writ to southern Lebanon, and winning U.S. praise. Rabin temporarily gained security for the Galilee and showed how effective the Israeli willingness to use force could be. In short, both states profited from their arrangement and, as Ze'ev Chafets pointed out, "Anytime Israel and Syria both emerge victorious from the same war, something new and different is happening in the Middle East."[4]

This event did more: American diplomats came away from Damascus saying that Assad recognized and accepted that to recover the Golan Heights he would have to reach a real peace with Israel, not just a minimal state of non-belligerency. In other words, the incident meant the Syrians discarded a fifth traditional formulation—non-

---

[1] Syrian Arab News Agency, October 27, 1991.

[2] Leslie Gelb, "Assad's Surprise," *New York Times*, March 4, 1993. Israeli sources perceived a much less drastic change (*Hadashot*, March 7, 1993; *Ha'aretz* March 9, 1993), but Gelb's account was apparently confirmed a week later when Foreign Minister Sharaa announced his government's willingness to accept a phased withdrawal (IDF Radio, March 11, 1993).

[3] Kol Yisra'el, February 27, 1993.

[4] Ze'ev Chafets, "Six-Day War II," *Jerusalem Report*, August 26, 1993.

belligerency, not peace—leading to some mild euphoria in Jerusalem. On the record, Israel's chief negotiator with Syria noted that "we have a serious partner—not only for negotiations, but also for an agreement."[1] Off the record, one of Rabin's top former aides confided, "we are convinced that Syria is. . . determined to reach an accord with us."[2] Another went further, saying that Christopher "laid the foundations for an Israeli-Syrian peace settlement."[3]

Knocked off track. Just days later, news of the Israeli-PLO Declaration of Principles came out and stopped the budding Israeli-Syrian progress cold. Israeli concentration on the Palestinian track, massive international attention to it, including a White House ceremony on September 13, 1993, and Assad's pique at being outmaneuvered (imagine, Arafat on the White House guest list, Assad on the State Department terrorism and drug trafficking lists) relegated Syrian-Israeli diplomacy to the side.

Negotiations then stalled for a full eight months. During this time, the Washington-based direct talks virtually ended, replaced by U.S. mediation. Other events (Basil al-Assad's death, the Hebron massacre) also intervened to delay progress between Syria and Israel. Israelis continued to complain about the Syrian offer (Peres: "it is an empty peace, devoid of content").[4] Two notable advances occurred during this period. First, Presidents Assad and Clinton met in Geneva on January 16, 1994. Although Syrian officials stressed how Assad used the meeting to reaffirm his pan-Arabist credentials,[5] the main headline from the summit was Assad's own announcement in a joint press conference with Clinton that the pursuit of peace was a "strategic choice" and that "in honor we shall make peace" with Israel. It was Clinton, however, who announced on Assad's behalf that Damascus was ready for "normal, peaceful relations" with Israel; Assad merely nodded in agreement.[6]

Second, Rabin sought to energize Syrian-Israeli talks by building on the momentum of the Clinton-Assad meeting and confirming his intent to move vigorously in negotiations. At the same time, he tried to

---

[1] IDF Radio, August 6, 1993.

[2] *Jerusalem Post International Edition*, August 14, 1993.

[3] *Yedi'ot Ahronot*, August 6, 1993.

[4] Agence France Presse, October 19, 1993.

[5] 'Abdullah al-Ahmar, assistant secretary general of the Ba'th Party, quoted Assad telling Clinton: "I do not differentiate between the Golan and southern Lebanon, between what is occupied from Palestine or Jordan. When I ask for one part, I ask for the whole" (Syrian Arab Republic Television, March 8, 1994).

[6] Judith Wrubel, ed., *Peacewatch: The Arab-Israeli Peace Process and U.S. Policy* (Washington, DC: The Washington Institute for Near East Policy, 1994), 181-83. This sequence prompted Charles Krauthammer to comment: "Why should the Israelis worry? Assad promises to be a good neighbor. They have Bill Clinton's word for it" (*Washington Post*, January 21, 1994).

defuse a growing mass movement in Israel protesting against a withdrawal from the Golan. He announced just one day after the Geneva summit his intent to call a national referendum before agreeing to a "significant withdrawal" of forces from the Golan Heights or to a dismantling of the settlements there. (Rabin subsequently explained that the referendum would ask, "Are you for or against a peace treaty with Syria?";[1] that it would precede any withdrawal, significant or not; and that it would follow the initialing of an agreement with Damascus but precede its signing.) News of the referendum met with severe criticism in official Damascus, perhaps because it much reduced the prime minister's freedom to move forward on his own. Although Assad had declared that "Rabin will lose his voters if he does not agree to a total withdrawal from the Golan," his regime sounded distinctly unhappy at the prospect of putting this assessment to the test ("We are not interested in Israeli polls").[2]

Indeed, total withdrawal had precious few supporters in Israel; a Jaffee Center for Strategic Studies poll in February 1993 showed only 6 percent of Israelis ready to return the entire Golan Heights in exchange for full contractual peace and diplomatic relations.[3] But the government's arguments made significant headway: 32 percent supported such a step in October 1994, 23 percent in December 1994, 37 percent in March 1995, 32 percent in May, 29 or 42 percent in June 1995, and 45 percent in November.[4] Still, the prospect of a referendum in Israel greatly increased Assad's burden: he had not just to win over the Labor party and its coalition allies but more than half the Israeli electorate.

"Withdrawal from the Golan Heights"

Impasse. Negotiations resumed in an indirect but more serious fashion in April 1994, as Rabin concentrated on the Syrian track.[5] The

---

[1] *Al Hamishmar*, September 19, 1994. Subsequently, Rabin slightly altered the referendum's wording: "Do you support this peace?" (Kol Yisra'el, October 3, 1994); "Are you for the peace treaty, knowing the price, knowing the setbacks, the security arrangements, or are you against it?" (*Jewish Exponent* [Philadelphia], July 14, 1995) or "Are you in favor of this peace or not?" (*Jerusalem Post*, August 11, 1995).

[2] Syrian Arab Television, November 23, 1992; see also interview with an unidentified "ranking" Syrian official, *al-Watan al-'Arabi*, September 16, 1994.

[3] *Davar*, February 23, 1993.

[4] October: *Jerusalem Post International Edition*, October 15, 1994; December: BESA Center poll; March: *Ha'aretz*, April 5, 1995; May: Steinmetz Center of Tel Aviv University, reported in *Ha'aretz*, July 2, 1995; June, 29 percent: Mina Tsemach, reported in *Jewish Exponent* (Philadelphia), June 9, 1995; June, 42 percent: Steinmetz Center of Tel Aviv University, reported in *Ha'aretz*, July 2, 1995; November: *Yedi'ot Ahronot*, December 1, 1995.

[5] Some Israelis perceived pressure from Washington. According to *Yedi'ot Ahronot*, April 1, 1994, "Clinton made it clear to Rabin: He wants a settlement with Syria, and fast. . . . The Americans nearly always support Israel in relation to the Palestinians, yet

Israelis responded with two initiatives: Rabin reportedly told a closed session of Israel's parliament on the nineteenth that he accepted a virtually full military withdrawal from the Golan, including the evacuation of all Israeli settlements;[1] and a few days later, when Secretary Christopher arrived in Israel, Rabin presented him with a detailed "peace package" to take to Damascus.

By bundling together its offer as a single package, Jerusalem hoped to steer the Syrians away from picking and choosing, but to no avail. Foreign Minister Sharaa derisively and undiplomatically dismissed parts of the plan as "silly" and "absurd."[2] Assad used equally pungent words. "The Israelis are dreaming," he reportedly told Lebanon's president, Ilyas al-Hirawi, about the notion of an eight-year withdrawal period.[3]

These comments irked the Israelis. Rabin quipped that if Assad's record "shows a readiness for peace on the part of Syria, then I don't know what opposition to peace would be."[4] Deputy Minister of Defense Mordechai Gur, now deceased, explained that "the Syrians are not ready yet to discuss any issue in detail—neither territory nor the nature of peace."[5] Rabin said he would make no more offers but await a positive reaction from Assad. As the weeks passed, he accused the Syrians of "playing for time" and called into doubt their being "serious about peace."[6] He warned Israelis that without an agreement with Syria, war would inevitably take place—and reduce funds available for social spending. Then Rabin turned around and warned Syrians that unless they were more forthcoming, he would ask for a large increase in military spending "to prepare [Israel] for war."[7] As his frustration grew, Rabin accused the Syrians of talking only to the U.S. government and "trying to ignore Israel."[8]

As spring 1994 turned into summer, Jerusalem and Damascus time and again called on the other to break the impasse. "Like two excessively polite guests," Raymond Cohen observes, they remained "locked in an endless debate about who is to enter the door first."[9]

Rabin found Clinton in a different mood in relation to the negotiations with al-Assad."

[1] Israel Television Channel Two, April 19, 1994; see also Kol Yisra'el, April 19, 1994; and *New York Times*, April 22, 1994.

[2] *Al-Hayat*, May 8, 1994. In the same spirit, Sharaa several months later dismissed Rabin's suggestion to solve the Lebanese impasse as a "practical joke" (*al-Hayat*, September 9, 1994).

[3] *Al-Shira'* (Beirut), July 4, 1994.

[4] *Al-Musawwar*, April 22, 1994.

[5] Educational Television Network (Tel Aviv), May 2, 1994.

[6] *Washington Post*, June 1, 1994.

[7] *Yedi'ot Ahronot*, June 29, 1994.

[8] *Al-Ahram*, July 18, 1994.

[9] Raymond Cohen, "Negotiations across the Golan Heights: Culture Gets in the Way," *Middle East Quarterly* (September 1994): 45.

Christopher undertook frequent visits to Syria and Israel, including marathon meetings with Assad, prompting wry humor comparing his efforts to a soap opera ("plenty of dialogue, a crisis just before the commercial, and a plot that never seems to budge").[1]

Though the two sides did make significant progress in their negotiations and maintained a range of mechanisms for communication, their leaders presented a publicly pessimistic face. Assad asserted that "So far, no significant progress has been achieved in the peace process," while his foreign minister flatly declared "There is no progress so far."[2] Rabin replied by noting that "gaps are still wide and deep" between the two states and held there "had still been no movement in Syria's inflexible position."[3] Peres stated that "the negotiations with Syria have not yet begun."[4]

Advances. Eventually, Christopher's efforts paid off. He convinced the two parties by August 1994 to put aside their basic disagreements over the extent of withdrawal and the definition of peace and focus instead on more immediate issues, such as those of security and timing. Hints of a Syrian peace plan emerged at this time; in addition, the two leaderships began to take incremental steps at public diplomacy, both to prepare their own publics to move from belligerency to peace and to convince the other side of their seriousness. Assad announced in a major speech on September 10 that "Syria shall meet the objective requirements of peace that are agreed upon."[5] Israeli and American officials responded enthusiastically. An American involved in the peace process called the latter statement "the most significant shift in Assad's public posture since [his decision to attend] the Madrid conference."[6] Israeli politicians received Assad's speech with unprecedented enthusiasm, using such terms as "very positive," "an important change in the atmosphere," and "an important and a positive speech."[7] Shimon Peres, ever the optimist, actually called it "a declaration of peace."[8]

The Israeli military responded less enthusiastically, however. Chief of Military Intelligence Major-General Uri Saguy—one of the earliest

---

[1] Steve Rodan, "Syria is Still Waiting for American Intervention," *Jerusalem Post International Edition*, August 13, 1994.

[2] Syrian Arab Television, September 10, 1994; Israeli Television Channel Two, October 1, 1994. The latter statement, it bears noting, is the first ever by a Syrian official spoken to Israeli television.

[3] On "gaps," see Kol Yisra'el, October 3, 1994; on "no movement," see IDF Radio, December 7, 1994.

[4] Kol Yisra'el, September 22, 1994.

[5] Syrian Arab Television, September 10, 1994.

[6] *New York Times*, October 16, 1994.

[7] Statements by the prime minister's bureau, Israeli Television Channel Two, September 10, 1994; see also Shimon Peres, Kol Yisra'el, September 11, 1994; and Itamar Rabinovich, IDF Radio, September 11, 1994.

[8] *Washington Post*, September 13, 1994.

advocates of exploring a potential strategic opening with Syria—explained with some disdain that "to the uninformed observer, Assad's speech would seem to include new elements. Those who regularly follow Assad, however, find in the speech confirmation of the assessment that Syria will do everything to exhaust the political process."[1]

The Israeli public's response to the whole effort was also lukewarm. When Syria's Foreign Minister Sharaa appeared on Israeli television for an unprecedented interview with an Israeli journalist, for example, many not only dismissed the theatrics as too little too late but also bristled at what Sharaa had to say. His reference to Jewish domination of the media and a flat denial that Syrian forces ever shelled Israeli residential areas from their pre-1967 position atop the Golan Heights did not sit well with Israelis.

Israeli columnist Yoel Marcus summed up a widespread Israeli feeling of disillusion:

> You know what? I'm fed up of seeing President Assad's sour face—his and that of his foreign minister, Faruq al-Sharaa. They behave, speak, and keep silent as if their very existence were a favor to us. They say a word or two, then rest for a month. They rest for a month and say another word. Then they rest again for a month. In between, the Assad experts here and in Washington closely interpret the poet's words.[2]

Arguing that Assad should stop "playing the prima donna" and instead "go out of his way to conquer our hearts," Marcus concludes that "the size of the [Israeli] concessions will be equal to the size of the smile [on Assad]."[3]

After these advances, negotiations stalled in late September. Faced with a closing window of opportunity, Bill Clinton took advantage of his presence at the signing of the Jordan-Israel peace treaty to pay a lightning visit to Damascus on October 27, 1994. Clinton later explained that he met with Assad "to say it's time he too followed the example and inspiration of Israel and Jordan."[4] Critics argued against giving Assad the political benefit from such a presidential visit—the first ever to a state on the State Department's terrorism list—and on a public level at least, the trip proved a major disappointment for the Americans.

At a joint press conference in Assad's presidential palace, the Syrian leader pointedly refused to condemn and renounce terrorism, as he evidently promised Clinton in private that he would. Hours later

---

[1] Kol Yisra'el, September 12, 1994.

[2] *Ha'aretz*, October 7, 1994.

[3] Ibid.

[4] "President Clinton's Saturday Radio Address," October 29, 1994, as transcribed by the Federal News Service.

in Jerusalem, an angry Clinton made Assad's statement on Assad's behalf, much like the "normal, peaceful relations" episode in Geneva nine months earlier. The administration strained to establish its accomplishments by alluding to private understandings (including a Syrian readiness to sign an initial pact in "four to six months")[1] and by overstating the significance of Assad's bristly public remarks. In one amusing incident, Christopher held that Assad's talk of establishing "peaceful, normal relations" with Israel broke new ground; he then "appeared taken aback" when shown that Clinton had reported the two presidents discussing "normal, peaceful relations" back in January.[2]

Still, Assad evidently did make some marginal concessions. In his meeting with Clinton, he reportedly agreed that Israeli withdrawal from the Golan could extend over eighteen months instead of twelve and that some elements of normalization could accompany the first stage of withdrawal. His most important concession was to agree in principle to Clinton's initiative that the private Israel-Syria talks in Washington be expanded to include not only the local ambassadors but also senior military officers, up to the rank of chief of staff.

After weeks of posturing and brinksmanship, the two chiefs of staff, Israel's Ehud Barak and Syria's Hikmat al-Shihabi, met in Washington during late December 1994 for ten hours of discussions over two days, culminating in an Oval Office session with President Clinton. In themselves, these unprecedented meetings marked an important development in the negotiations: for Assad to send his top soldier marked a quantum leap in the level of representation at peace talks and signaled the seriousness of his intent to both Jerusalem and Washington. Further, that Assad dispatched Shihabi, a man regarded as pro-Western in orientation (because of his role in negotiating the 1974 disengagement agreement and his sending his son to the United States for university training) reinforced the impression that Assad was keen to improve his relationship with the United States.

In substance, however, the meetings achieved little. Israel's ambassador to the United States, Itamar Rabinovich, later characterized his government as having "failed carefully to prepare" for them, so that they took place "almost spontaneously."[3] Among other points raised, Barak called for a reduction in the size of the Syrian armed forces, a demilitarized zone in Syria nine times larger than one to be established in Israel (a reflection of the two countries' land areas), and the joint use of early warning stations. The Syrians not only outright rejected these suggestions but reports from Damascus indicated that Assad found such demands (especially the reduction in

---

[1]   *Washington Times*, October 28, 1994.

[2]   *New York Times*, October 28, 1994; see also *Philadelphia Inquirer*, October 30, 1994; for the January 1994 statement, see Wrubel, *Peacewatch*, 183, 187.

[3]   *Davar*, June 30, 1995.

troop levels) "humiliating" and reflecting an Israeli intention to destabilize his regime.[1]

Stalled. The talks did not lead to further progress. Rather, Assad broke off direct negotiations with Israel during the first half of 1995 and reverted back to indirect talks via the Americans. Assad rebuffed repeated Israeli calls for a summit meeting of the two leaders, deeming this premature. In a noteworthy commentary, he told a visiting foreign minister that Sadat was assassinated "not because he made peace with Israel but because of the shameful way he behaved; for instance by addressing the Knesset [Israel's parliament]." Assad concluded that he would "not agree to meet with any Israeli leader as long as occupied Syrian land is in Israeli hands."[2]

This lull left Israelis and Americans speculating about Assad's motives and about the possibility of concluding a Syria-Israel treaty in the foreseeable future. Peres saw the Syrian president in a conundrum, being someone who "has divorced war but has not yet married peace. Al-Assad is now a strategic bachelor."[3] The U.S. government's Special Middle East Coordinator Dennis Ross reportedly speculated that Assad purposefully slowed down the negotiations to devote his energy to domestic affairs, and especially to promoting his son Bashshar.

Though negotiations had shut down, the Israeli side made some concessions. Rabin indicated a readiness to make a withdrawal "more symbolic than geographic," offering to pull back from one Israeli settlement even before a full agreement with Syria.[4] Peres declared at one point that "The Golan Heights is Syrian land, and we are sitting on the Syrians' land," adding shortly after that "The Golan Heights was never historically considered a part of the State of Israel."[5] Rabin then went further and declared that "Neither [Theodor] Herzl nor any other of Israel's founders of any stripe ever dreamt the Golan Heights would be part of the state of Israel."[6]

---

[1] *Ma'ariv*, April 30, 1995.

[2] Guido de Marco of Malta, *Ha'aretz*, February 12, 1995. Israelis speculated that his real reason was a fear of leaks, while Egyptians pointed to his actually believing in stereotypes about "devious Jews" and worrying about being outsmarted (*Davar*, August 1, 1994).

[3] Israeli Television Channel One, February 6, 1995; see also *al-Hayat*, February 19, 1995.

[4] Israeli Television Channel One, May 26, 1995.

[5] *Yedi'ot Ahronot*, May 28, 1995; see also Israel Television Channel One, June 2, 1995.

[6] *Washington Times*, June 28, 1995. Matters are not so cut and dried. The first Zionist settlement on the Golan Heights was established in 1886, followed by a number of others, supported by one of Israel's great early founders, Baron Edmund de Rothschild. Further, the area was included in the Land of Israel as defined by the Zionist delegation to the Paris Peace Conference in 1919. It became part of the French mandate for Syria only when the British ceded it in 1923. Zionist attempts to buy land lasted into the 1930s.

Under pressure from the U.S. government, Assad finally relented and agreed to resume the direct talks in late June 1995, when the two chiefs of staff sat down for a second round of talks. They agreed in principle on the need for a demilitarized zone, a thinned-out zone, an infrastructure for early-warning, and confidence-building measures; but in every case they disagreed on the specifics, leading Israel's Chief of Staff Amnon Shahak to describe the gap between the parties as "very wide."[1]

Although Assad had agreed to follow the chief of staff talks with lower-level military meetings, he suddenly required an Israeli concession (not to demand early warning stations on the Golan Heights) before returning soldiers to the table; in the meantime, he offered only to resume the ambassadorial talks. The Israelis adamantly refused to accept the new condition for, as Prime Minister Rabin explained, "If they do not fulfill the understanding achieved on this issue, who can ensure us that they will fulfill other obligations in the future?"[2] Rabin also refused to resume the ambassadorial talks. Backing up the Israeli position, Secretary of State Christopher insisted that Assad send a military delegation to Washington, without results.

Again the talks closed down for six months. Rabin let it be known he no longer expected to reach a final agreement with Assad before his own term of office ended (that is, by the next Israeli election, which must be held no later than October 29, 1996). The Israeli press speculated that Assad became ill and had cut down on his work; government circles suspected Assad suffered from "cold feet"; Rabin thought it had to do with his profound misunderstanding of the democratic system; and Dennis Ross was said to think Assad slowed things down to avoid falling into the Palestinian shadow.[3] And so matters remained—stagnant, barbed, and in danger of breaking down altogether—for four months, until the assassination of Yitzhak Rabin on November 4, 1995.

Because Rabin's death led to Shimon Peres becoming prime minister, it had the unintended consequence of greatly spurring Syrian-Israeli negotiations. Immediately on coming to office, Peres made a significant, if subtle, concession to Assad; he dropped Rabin's insistence on the military format and offered a quite different package: higher-level diplomatic officials to meet in a secluded setting over periods of many days, with the Americans a full participant. Secretary Christopher traveled to Damascus in December and won Assad's quick agreement to this procedure, which was set to begin during the final days of 1995. In addition, hoping to appeal to Assad's vanity, Peres depicted a Syrian-Israeli peace as the effective end of the Arab-Israeli

---

[1]   IDF Radio, June 30, 1995.

[2]   *Ha'aretz,* July 18, 1995.

[3]   Ibid., August 1, 1995.

conflict; to dramatize this, in a speech before Congress, he raised the prospect of an all-Middle East summit meeting (excluding only the Libyan, Sudanese, Iraqi, and Iranian leaders) that would seal a region-wide peace.[1] Peres and his aides hinted at concessions in matters of substance as well, such as the timetable of withdrawal and the requirements for security arrangements.

Seeing peace with Syria as the key to ending the historic conflict on Israel's borders, the Peres government limited its demands to those directly affecting Israeli security on the Golan and in southern Lebanon and apparently did not include many other possible issues, including: Syrian troop withdrawal from the Bekaa Valley;[2] limits on Syria's force structure or arsenal; restrictions on the placing of Syrian forces outside of the force-limitation areas; ending the anti-Israel rhetoric in the media; a total shut-down of Syrian support for terrorism; restrictions on Syrian activities *vis-à-vis* Turkey; the expulsion of Western criminals from Syria; the permanent settlement of some 300,000 Palestinians resident in Syria; the return of Ron Arad, an Israeli airman lost in the 1982 war; Israeli leasing of land on the Golan Heights; or an Israeli deterrent force remaining on the Heights in perpetuity.

Assessing the Negotiations

Two offers. The terms of the Israeli offer first made in May 1994 have changed and developed over time; drawing on Israeli government statements, press reports, and Likud Party statements, here follows an outline of that offer as it had evolved by December 1995. Israel would:

• Recognize as Israel's future border with Syria the international frontier demarcated by the British and French in 1923. For Israel, this frontier is preferable to the June 4, 1967 border, because it leaves two key geographic features in Israel's control: the Golan's 500-meter high northwestern cliffs and a large chunk of the country's water resources;[3]

• Withdraw all its troops to this border in stages over a maximum three-year period, with the first stage to include the transfer of three Druze villages (Majd al-Shams, Buq'ata, and Sa'da) to Syrian control

---

[1] *Mideast Mirror*, December, 13, 1995.

[2] Itamar Rabinovich characterizes a Syrian pullout from Lebanon as "not an Israeli issue but an international issue" and notes that his government "does not presume to speak on behalf of the entire international community. . . . We do not demand a Syrian pullout as a condition for an arrangement" (IDF Radio, November 2, 1994). Tacit Israeli acceptance of the status quo leaves France as the only power reluctant to acknowledge the Syrian occupation of Lebanon, a point then-Foreign Minister Alain Juppé took pains to make in an interview to *al-Hayat*, September 14, 1994.

[3] Rabin was reported to say that for him a pullback from "98 percent" of the Golan Height's land constituted "a withdrawal from the Golan" (*Ma'ariv*, February 9, 1995); in other words, retracting Israeli troops to the international line would be a partial withdrawal. To confuse matters further, he then denied this statement (*Ma'ariv*, February 10, 1995).

(accordingly, the plan is sometimes called Majd al-Shams First) and perhaps the evacuation of one Israeli settlement;

- Evacuate all thirty-two Israeli settlements on the Golan Heights with 13,000 residents, also in stages;
- Recognize Syria's "special relationship" with Lebanon;
- Permit one or two Syrian early-warning stations on a mountain top in Israel's Galilee region; and
- Demilitarize a small area of the Jordan Rift Valley.

In return, the Syrians would:

- Implement full normalization after the first stage of withdrawal, which Rabin described as "an Israeli Embassy in Damascus, a Syrian Embassy in Israel, an [Israeli] bus traveling to Aleppo, Israeli tourists in Homs, Israeli ships at Tartus, El Al planes landing at Syrian airports, and commercial and cultural ties—everything, and in both directions";[1]
- Demilitarize the Golan Heights and the territory reaching almost the whole way to Damascus; in this roughly fifty kilometer strip the Syrian government may station only lightly-armed police;
- Create a "thinning-out strip" of another fifty or so kilometers in which Syrian forces and armaments will be limited to specified maximums and traffic can only travel along paved roads;
- Accept American monitoring of treaty compliance;
- Accede to an Israeli lookout post on Mt. Hermon, electronic monitors on the Golan Heights, and electronic devices at the gates of military bases housing tanks;
- Agree to various confidence-building measures such as a hot line, advance notification of military exercises and maneuvers, an exchange of military observers, joint patrols along the border and joint participation in the United Nations observer force, and Syria's joining new regional security frameworks;
- Guarantee that Israel continue, via the Sea of Galilee, to receive an agreed-upon share of Golan waters; and that these waters not be contaminated;
- Cancel Syria's participation in anti-Israel alliances and pacts;
- Stop attacks by Hezbollah and various Palestinian groups from southern Lebanon; and permit the Lebanese Army to control it.

At other times, Rabin reportedly stated that Israel's withdrawal on the Golan Heights also required the disbanding of all the Palestinian organizations based in Damascus. Also, according to a senior Israeli official, Rabin was unwilling to make concessions until he met with Assad.[2] (To which Assad reportedly replied, "I'd rather lose my arm than shake the hand of an Israeli.")[3]

---

[1] Kol Yisra'el, October 3, 1994.

[2] *Jerusalem Report*, August 11, 1994.

[3] *Jerusalem Post International Edition*, October 8, 1994. Assad reportedly said something similar to Egypt's Hosni Mubarak: "There will be no handshake with Rabin. I would

In addition, as a way to appeal to Assad's desire to improve on the Sadat model of peacemaking, Peres has depicted peace with Syria as effectively ending the Arab-Israeli conflict and has sought to arrange an all-Middle East summit (without the Libyan, Iraqi, Iranian, and Sudanese leaders) to symbolize the end of the conflict.[1]

At the same time, the Israeli package does not directly address a number of Syrian wishes, including eliminating the Israel nuclear arsenal and infrastructure or a resettlement in Israel of Palestinians resident in Syria (nearly all of whom arrived as a result of the war in 1948-49).

In August 1994, the media published details of a Syrian peace plan. Less elaborated than the Israeli version, it merely offers normal and natural relations (the Syrian locution for "normalize relations") with Israel in return for Jerusalem taking a range of steps:

• Recognize the June 4, 1967 border between Israel and Syria,[2] and demarcate it as the future border;

• Remove all Israeli citizens and withdraw all Israeli forces beyond that border before the next Israeli elections (i.e., no later than October 29, 1996), with the first phase to include the dismantling of at least one Israeli settlement;

• Permit Syrian forces to return to the armistice lines without limits on their numbers or armaments;

• Abrogate the 1981 decision to apply Israeli law to the Golan Heights;

• Implement nearly symmetrical security provisions for both sides;

• Accept international forces to monitor the accord;

• Postpone the establishment of diplomatic relations until after the completion of full Israeli withdrawal;

• Accept a joint Syrian-Lebanese negotiating team and not interfere in the "special" Syrian-Lebanese relationship; and

• Delink the issue of southern Lebanon from the Golan Heights.

Four legs. Despite the many differences between the two sides—as well as the public atmosphere of skepticism and recrimination—they appear to have established the general contours of an agreement. Following Rabin's metaphor of a table standing on four legs, their differences amount to the following manageable areas:

• *Extent of withdrawal.* The Israelis have indicated in a number of indirect ways that, in the context of an overall agreement and subject to a national referendum, they would be willing to return roughly to the international (or Mandatory) border delineated in March 1923.

---

rather cut my hand off" (*Der Spiegel,* August 8, 1994).

[1] See Peres's speech to a joint session of Congress, *Mideast Mirror,* December 13, 1995.

[2] It bears noting that three distinct boundaries exist to the west of the Golan Heights: the Mandatory border (1923-1948), the armistice lines of 1949, and the actual border that existed from 1949 until June 4, 1967. In the third case, demilitarized zones took up some seven square miles (eighteen square kilometers).

Shimon Peres made this most explicit when he accepted the "international line" as the border.[1] Rabin himself refused to issue a statement to this effect in advance of an overall agreement for tactical reasons: "If I make such an announcement publicly, in a binding way," Rabin told an interviewer, "what will happen to my bargaining chips?"[2] After becoming prime minister, Peres adopted a similar caution. Asked at a press conference during a December 1995 visit to Washington, why he hesitates to offer to "give up all of the Golan Heights," Peres replied: "I don't hesitate. I think the time didn't come yet for me to announce it."[3]

For Assad, a decision to accept an Israeli offer of withdrawal to the Mandatory lines would mark a retreat from his demand for total withdrawal to the June 4, 1967 border and would open him to accusations of having failed to win for Syria what Sadat won back at Camp David. However, Assad could obscure the issue if he found some artful way to accept Israel's offer, like Jordan's "lease-back" formula for Israeli farmers on Jordanian sovereign territory, or an exchange of territories, as Damascus and Baghdad recently agreed to as a way to settle their outstanding border dispute.[4]

The difference between the Mandatory and June 4, 1967 borders amounts to twenty-five square miles (sixty-five square kilometers). The June 4, 1967 border lies further west than the Mandatory one mainly in four places, all to the benefit of Syria: (1) an area including the Banyas River, a main tributary of the Jordan River; (2) the village of al-Hamma, a less-than-one square kilometer enclave captured by Jordanian troops in 1948 and subsequently handed over to Syria;[5] (3) several hundred meters running along the east bank of the Jordan River; (4) a ten-meter wide strip along the shore of Lake Tiberias.

Though small in area, these four regions have hydraulic as well as symbolic importance. Banyas supplies 12 percent of the Jordan River;

---

[1] Israeli Television Channel One, April 18, 1995. Peres immediately claimed to have been misunderstood; he had intended only to mention that a 1967 Israeli government resolution called for a peace treaty with Syria "based on the international border" (*Ma'ariv*, April 18, 1995). Other Israeli politicians were more explicit, such as Minister of the Environment Yossi Sarid: "The price that Israel will have to pay for full peace is known. . . a full withdrawal from the Golan Heights" (*Philadelphia Inquirer*, June 12, 1995). Finance Minister Avraham Shohat said "almost all the territory" would have to go back to Syria (IDF Radio June 13, 1995). Israel's President Ezer Weizman stated that the Labor government is inclined to withdraw to the Mandatory border.

[2] *Yedi'ot Ahronot*, October 28, 1994.

[3] Federal News Service transcript of a National Press Club meeting, December 12, 1995.

[4] *Mideast Mirror*, December 18, 1995.

[5] Al-Hamma (the Biblical Hammat Gader), it bears noting, had been considered part of the Golan Heights before the Mandatory period. See, for example, G. Schumacher, *The Jaulân* (London: Richard Bentley and Son, 1888), 149-60, which provides an extremely detailed description of the village.

al-Hamma gives Syria potential rights to the Yarmuk River; land along the Jordan River strengthens Syrian claims to its waters; and shore along Lake Tiberias provides the basis for staking a claim to the lake waters. Israelis tend to see the protection of water sources on the Golan as no less vital than military issues. Ze'ev Schiff calls it the "paramount" concern, while Rabin had been quoted as saying that "the greatest danger Israel has to face in the negotiations with Syria is the possibility of losing control over the Golan Heights water resources."[1]

In the end, there is a strong possibility that Assad will not insist on the June 4, 1967 borders, even though this is what UN Security Council Resolution 242 implicitly calls for. The territory involved is too small to break a Syrian-Israeli deal. Also, doing so requires Assad to fall back on the prerogative of military conquest, an argument that opens the way for the Israelis to claim the whole of the Golan. Should the two sides reach agreement, it will probably be on the 1923 border, with some adjustments in Israel's favor.[2]

• *Timetable of withdrawal.* Jerusalem started with a target of eight years in three stages while Damascus spoke of a full withdrawal over six months. By the beginning of 1995, the one side had gone down to four years and the other increased to eighteen months. Since then, trial balloons floated from Israel have hinted at an even shorter period.[3] A compromise—akin to the three-year Sinai withdrawal outlined in the Egypt-Israel agreement—seems likely.

• *Security arrangements* (i.e., preventing a surprise attack, the Israeli military's great nightmare since 1973). The Golan Heights have great

---

[1] Ze'ev Schiff, *Peace With Security: Israel's Minimal Security Requirements in Negotiations with Syria*, Policy Paper Number Thirty-Four (Washington, DC: The Washington Institute for Near East Policy, 1993), 90; Rabin in *Ma'ariv*, July 19, 1995.

[2] Further complicating matters, in July 1995 the PLO put in a claim for what it called the "Palestinian Golan." What area it laid claim to is not clear, sometimes only the area of al-Hamma, at other times "a band of 360 square kilometers" (144 square miles) that would give Palestinians a claim on water rights (Agence France Presse, July 24 and 26, 1995).

The claim to al-Hamma is not new; indeed, the original Palestine National Covenant of 1964 mentioned the "area of al-Hamma" along with the West Bank and Gaza, implicitly portraying it as an area of Palestine not under Israeli control (the 1968 version dropped this reference). Yasser Arafat correctly points out about al-Hamma that "the Syrians made a gift of it to Ahmad Shukeiri [the PLO chairman of that time] so that he could set up his Palestinian state there (Agence France Presse, July 26, 1995); the offer went unheeded, but it does establish Syrian recognition of a Palestinian claim.

For Syria, Defense Minister Mustafa Tallas rejected the PLO claim: "This is the first time the term 'Palestinian Golan' has been heard. The Golan is known to be Syrian" (Radio Lebanon, August 2, 1995). For Israel, Shimon Peres rejected a Palestinian claim to al-Hamma on the grounds that "it is difficult to talk about Palestinian rights, because there never was a Palestinian state" (*Jordan Times*, July 29, 1995). In contrast, the Egyptian government apparently endorses the PLO claim (indeed, in a surprise move, President Mubarak was the one first to announce its bid).

[3] *Mideast Mirror*, December 18, 1995.

practical value to Israel (to see and hear what goes on in Syria; to prevent Syrians from knowing what goes on in Israel; to have for Israeli forces and to deny to the Syrian ones) and great symbolic value to Assad (who lost them in 1967). On the question of demilitarization, the Syrians began with a call for exact symmetry while the Israelis sought a nine-to-one ratio on either side of the border. By mid-1995, the Syrians offered a ten-to-six ratio and the bargaining was underway.

The issue of Israel's maintaining an early warning station or two on Mt. Hermon remains highly contentious. Rabin declared that "on this issue there will be no compromise,"[1] while Assad made it equally clear he had to have all Israelis off the Golan. With the exception of an errant broadcast on July 10, 1995, when a Syrian Arab Republic Radio commentary stated that "it would be possible to assign this task to international and friendly forces," Damascus steadfastly refused to permit any kind of station, even in the face of an Israeli offer of one or two Syrian stations on Israel territory. Assad did hint, however, that he might accept Israeli airborne surveillance. Several indications suggested that Assad's refusal to countenance a station on the mountain may have less to do with military secrets than political ones. He was quoted as saying that "Syrian monitoring in Safed is less crucial than my opposition to an Israeli presence on Mt. Hermon."[2] Assad was also quoted saying that the Israeli presence on the Golan Heights "burns me night and day."[3] That's not hard to understand, for the big Israel ear humiliates the otherwise all-mighty Syrian leadership:

> Behind the anonymous facade of the Presidential Palace in Damascus, Hafez Assad and his closest colleagues have invented a new language to confuse the enemy. Instead of the ebb and flow of discussion that characterizes Cabinet meetings in other countries, Mr. Assad's ministers have become experts in using hand signals—a sign language reserved for sensitive issues that is meant to confuse the Mossad agents who eavesdrop on every whisper in the corridors of power. . . . Just 20 miles from the heart of Damascus, Israel's military intelligence has installed electronic gear capable of recording the most intimate conversations at the palace.[4]

• *Normalization.* Jerusalem demands full normalization after the first stage of withdrawal. Assad initially refused to give any details about normalization, saying this would follow after a complete withdrawal. With time, he made two concessions. First, he hinted that Israel would receive much of what it sought, talking on one occasion about "normal peace, of the type existing between 187 countries in the world"[5] and on

---

[1]   *Ha'aretz,* July 21, 1995.

[2]   *Yedi'ot Ahronot,* May 26, 1995.

[3]   Quoted by an unnamed visitor, *Jerusalem Post International Edition*, October 8, 1994.

[4]   *Washington Times,* August 17, 1994.

[5]   Hafez al-Assad, speaking to Representative Tom Lantos, *Yedi'ot Ahronot,* January 15, 1995. This passage is translated back to English from Hebrew.

another about "good relations with Israel, like Egypt and Jordan have."[1] Second, he agreed to establish low-level diplomatic relations after the first, partial withdrawal of Israeli forces.

In addition to these areas of agreement, there has been another positive sign. Despite both sides insisting that no behind-the-scenes discussions were taking place, evidence points to at least four unpublicized sets of talks. In the first channel, sponsored from May 1992 by the Washington-based Search for Common Ground, non-governmental figures from Syria and Israel met in European capitals and hashed through issues in detail, perhaps supplying the drafts of a settlement. The second talks took place under Egyptian auspices, starting in August 1992. They featured 'Isa Darwish, the Syrian ambassador to Egypt, and Nimrod Novik, a former Peres aide still close to his old boss. This track resulted in one dramatic result: a telephone call between Peres and Sharaa in September 1992.[2]

The third discussions took place in Washington under U.S. government auspices, with the two chief negotiators—Israel's Itamar Rabinovich and Syria's Walid al-Moualem—meeting quietly some dozens of times since May 1994 in U.S. government buildings and in the private homes of participants. Some meetings included Christopher, others had high-ranking officials flown in from the Middle East. Observers credited these discussions with developing small advances which kept the negotiations from deadlock.[3] The fourth track took place in London, where businessmen and academics from the two sides met on an occasional basis; what made these gatherings of greater interest was the reported participation of Shimon Peres for Israel and of children of Syrian regime leaders, including Faris, the son of Rif'at al-Assad, and Falak, the daughter of Mustafa Tallas.

Reflections

Differences. Several basic differences separate the two sides. First, Jerusalem sees the Golan Heights almost exclusively in practical terms: security, water sources, and the pain of resettling thousands of residents dominate its discourse. In contrast, while Damascus does refer to the strategic advantage that control of the Heights gives to Israel, it mostly focuses on regaining the Golan as a matter of national pride. One side talks facts, the other symbols. But, on closer inspection, the stress on pride also has to do with national security—not external threats but domestic stability: the Alawi regime needs to prove its nationalist credentials to the Sunni majority, and regaining the Golan

---

[1] *Ha'aretz,* February 12, 1995.

[2] *Al-Bilad* (Amman), November 9, 1994; see also *Jerusalem Post International Edition,* December 10, 1994.

[3] Kol Yisra'el, September 19, 1994; see also *L'Express,* October 6, 1994; and *New York Times,* December 31, 1994.

Heights offers it the best way to do so. While both sides are talking about security, then, they worry about markedly different kinds of threats.

Second, Israel's position capitalizes on its military victory in 1967 ("Syria made a mistake when it attacked us and this is the price of its mistake"), while Syria's seeks to ignore that victory and stress the justice of its cause ("The Golan has been Syrian territory since time immemorial").[1] Pithy statements by leaders sum up this difference: Rabin asserted that "the depth of withdrawal will match the depth of peace."[2] In contrast, Sharaa notes that if it took Israel only six days to occupy the Golan Heights, it can evacuate the area just as quickly.

Third, though the talks are nominally about the disposition of the Golan Heights, that issue is secondary to the real objective of each party—for Israel, to make peace and end the military conflict on its borders; for Syria, to develop a new relationship with Washington. These different goals profoundly shape attitudes toward an accord: while Israelis talk impatiently of wrapping up a deal in so many weeks or months, Damascus indicates it has all the time in the world because the U.S. involvement in the process further deepens with every passing negotiation. Israelis point out that leaders could disappear from power any day (through natural causes, election, or assassination) and stress the need for quick action. In contrast Assad affirms "We are not in a hurry" about reaching an agreement;[3] he has also said that if this generation cannot reach an agreement, the next one can do so; and that "Reconciliation is not possible in my generation."[4]

Ordinary countries. Both Israel and Syria have had outsized roles in Middle Eastern and world politics. By signing a peace agreement, both would lose importance internationally. Israelis, who crave normality, welcome the prospect of stopping the endless rounds of war, of their state recognized by the neighbors, and of no longer being haunted by terrorism. They would gladly leave behind the battles still working out the legacy of World War I and instead focus their energies on the marketplace of the twenty-first century.

With Assad, the calculation is more complicated. On one hand, he may view peace as an opportunity to create a new role for Syria as a constructive regional power. In an era of peace, Syria could present itself to Washington as the guarantor of security on four of Israel's fronts—Lebanese, Syrian, Jordanian, and Palestinian—and so compete

---

[1]   Shimon Peres, *Akhbar al-Yawm*, September 17, 1994; see also Syrian Arab Republic Radio, May 28, 1994.

[2]   *Ha'aretz*, December 17, 1993.

[3]   Syrian Arab Republic Radio, March 12, 1992. Although Rabin sometimes spoke similarly ("We've been on the Golan Heights for twenty-seven years, and we can happily stay there for another twenty-seven," *Jerusalem Report*, July 14, 1994), his record belies this proclaimed patience.

[4]   *Der Spiegel*, August 8, 1994.

with Egypt for paramountcy among America's Arab allies. On the other hand, Assad may believe that peace diminishes Syria's strategic relevance. Peter Rodman points out that peace with Israel means Damascus "will no longer be able to play its Palestinian card, or its terrorism card, and risks its Iranian card—the very things on which it has always relied to serve its leadership ambitions in the Arab world. With peace, Syria is an ordinary country."[1] Though Syria would gain U.S. patronage, getting back the Golan Heights might in fact weaken its strength in Middle Eastern politics—not at all a welcome prospect.

What does Assad intend? On May 24, 1966, very soon after becoming minister of defense and a full year before Syria lost the Golan Heights, Hafez al-Assad had this to say about relations with Israel: "We shall never call for, nor accept peace. We shall only accept war and the restoration of the usurped land [i.e., Israel proper]. We have resolved to drench this land with our blood, to oust you, aggressors, and throw you into the sea for good."[2] Assad would no longer, it hardly needs emphasis, make such a statement; recalling it points up just how much his policy toward Israel has changed over the decades.

He has overseen an evolution in Syrian policy from outright military confrontation to a more nuanced conflict involving diplomacy as well as armed force. It is difficult, however, to determine whether this portends a gradual acceptance of Israel or merely a more subtle way of trying to eliminate it, whether Assad intends to use diplomacy to make real peace or merely to buy time, and whether his changes strategic or tactical. The evidence supports contrary interpretations. Double games, tough bargaining, and the obscurity of Syrian public opinion make it particularly difficult to assess Assad's intentions.

The three Israeli leaders quoted in the epigraph demonstrate the range of opinion about Assad's intentions, and they are hardly the only ones to disagree. On the optimistic side, Uri Saguy, head of Israeli military intelligence in 1992-95, sees a "pragmatic acceptance of Israel"; Yossi Olmert, a member of Likud's negotiating team with Syria, likewise refers to "Syria's change of heart" *vis-à-vis* Israel: "the subject of negotiations has shifted from whether to make a deal at all to settling on the price."[3] Ehud Ya'ari, one of Israel's leading interpreters of Arab politics, writes that "the Syrians know they don't have any real choice other than to fit into the peace structure that is shaping up."[4]

The U.S. government has no doubt that Syrian policy toward Israel has changed. Martin Indyk, then on the National Security Council

---

[1]   Peter W. Rodman, "Waiting for Assad," *New Republic*, August 8, 1994.

[2]   Quoted by Abba Eban, *Jerusalem Post*, June 20, 1967.

[3]   *Yedi'ot Ahronot*, September 14, 1993; see also Yossi Olmert, *Toward a Syrian-Israeli Peace Agreement: Perspective of a Former Negotiator*, Policy Focus Number Twenty-Five (Washington, DC: The Washington Institute for Near East Policy, 1994), 20-21.

[4]   *Jerusalem Report*, September 8, 1994.

staff, stated in November 1993 that "Assad has made a strategic decision to make peace with Israel."[1] Two months later, after meeting with Assad, President Clinton was asked if he felt the Syrian leader had made a firm commitment to normalize relations with Israel. Without hesitation, he replied "The short answer is yes."[2] Later that same day, he further elaborated: "I think that he [Assad] has reached a conclusion that it is in the interests of his people, his administration and his legacy to make a meaningful and lasting peace."[3] Even more optimistically, Clinton observed after a trip to Damascus in October 1994 that "something is changing in Syria. Its leaders realize it is time to make peace."[4]

Other analysts are more skeptical. The *Washington Post* editorialized that "It is not at all clear that it means more to [Assad] to play the nationalist and reclaim the Golan than to play the militant and keep using the territory as an issue demonstrating Syria's anti-Israel defiance."[5] Barry Rubin writes that "a 'no war, no peace' situation—perhaps with new safeguards—would seem more attractive to Syria than a diplomatic resolution capped by a peace treaty and mutual recognition."[6] Ahmad Jibril of the Popular Front for the Liberation of Palestine-General Command, an enemy of the Israeli-Palestinian peace accords, agrees.

> I do not think the Syrian leadership will sign an agreement with the Israelis like the agreements signed with King Hussein, Yasser Arafat, or the one signed at Camp David. . . . I will be astonished if—God forbid—the Israeli flag is hoisted in the Damascus sky. . . . An agreement ending the state of war may be signed and a sort of truce may be reached. . . . I think the Syrian leadership will eventually prefer the fighting or war option—whatever other circumstances may be—rather than accepting the U.S.-Israeli peace.[7]

Moshe Ma'oz held in 1992 that "on the most essential points, Syria has not changed its positions."[8] Perhaps the most pungent assessment came from Jesse Helms, chairman of the Senate Foreign Relations Committee, who declared the Syria-Israel peace process a "fraud" because "Syria doesn't want peace. . . . They want access to the

---

[1]   Martin Indyk, "Perspectives from the White House," *Middle East Quarterly* (March 1994): 62.

[2]   *New York Times*, January 17, 1994.

[3]   Wrubel ed., *Peacewatch*, 187.

[4]   Speech to Israel's parliament, *Weekly Compilation of Presidential Documents* (U.S. Government Printing Office, October 31, 1994).

[5]   *Washington Post*, May 18, 1994.

[6]   Barry Rubin, *Radical Middle East States and U.S. Policy*, Policy Paper Number Thirty-Five (Washington, DC: The Washington Institute for Near East Policy, 1993), 38.

[7]   *Al-Wasat*, November 14-20, 1994.

[8]   Moshe Ma'oz, "Syrian-Israeli Relations and the Middle East Peace Process," *Jerusalem Journal of International Relations* 14 (1992): 12.

pocketbooks of the American taxpayers."[1] But the most suspicious interpretation came from Avigdor Haselkorn, who speculated in late 1991 that Syrian participation in the peace process could prepare for a military strike by improving Assad's standing in the West. "If his plan is successful," Haselkorn wrote, Assad "will in due course be in a position to make a military push into the Golan Heights, perhaps with tacit international backing."[2]

Within Israeli military intelligence, disagreement over Assad's intentions raged so fiercely between two senior figures, then-Chief of Intelligence Uri Saguy and his deputy, Ya'acov Ami-Dror, that the 1995 annual evaluation could not go to press on time. Such intense disagreement reflects the fact that we know too little to judge Assad's intentions. Indeed, we do not even know that Assad himself has made up his mind; having entered into negotiations as a means to improve relations with Washington, he could well have no real sense of their outcome. Further, if Assad sticks to form, he will likely keep his options open. And he may not decide whether to accept a negotiated agreement until he sees the final details, as happened in December 1973. (He bargained hard at that time with Henry Kissinger over every detail of the U.S.- and Soviet-sponsored Geneva conference, including the date and even the wording of the invitation; only after the negotiations were successfully concluded did he inform Kissinger that he had no intention of having his government attend.)

Israelis pay much heed to Assad's reluctance, for they place great emphasis on confidence-building measures: that, after all, is much of what they receive in return from their withdrawal from strategically important territory. Rabin noted that Assad had not accomplished 1 or 2 percent of what Sadat had done to convince Israelis of his sincerity. (To which, the Syrians reply, accurately, that "President Sadat is not President Assad.")[3] Some Israelis believe that a grudging peace treaty with Damascus is simply not worth the price. The leader of Israel's opposition party, Benjamin Netanyahu, goes further and concludes that "we will end up with a peace treaty on paper while Syria will get the Golan"; to that he says, "no deal."[4] Ariel Sharon, the former defense minister and leading hawk, says he prefers the Golan Heights without peace to peace without the Golan Heights.

Why does Assad risk peace with Israel? Whatever Assad's precise intentions, the possibility now exists that Jerusalem could concede a bit

---

[1] Cable News Network, November 19, 1994.

[2] Avigdor Haselkorn, "Assad Commentary," *American Spectator*, October 1991, 24.

[3] "Syrian Foreign Minister Farouk al-Sharaa Reaffirms Peace for Golan Withdrawal," *Middle East Insight* (November-December 1994): 15.

[4] Kol Yisra'el, November 21, 1993. Yoash Tsiddon-Chatto, a Likud politician, put it even more strongly: "a piece of paper cannot substitute for a mountain range" (*Jerusalem Report*, December 1, 1994). See also Kol Yisra'el, May 27, 1995.

more—a prospect even more likely with Shimon Peres rather than Yitzhak Rabin as prime minister[1]—so that Damascus would find it difficult not to sign a peace treaty. Does Assad, having permitted the situation to reach this point of potential breakthrough, in fact intend to reach an agreement with Israel?

Assad's actions can be read in two contrary ways: either to suggest that he seeks a lasting peace with Israel, or that he wants only to *appear* to seek such a peace. Considering the evidence, the latter is more likely the case.

Though Assad has reportedly said that peace with Israel will strengthen Alawi rule,[2] the end of anti-Zionism could actually be more risky than continued confrontation. Many of his key constituencies appear intensely to dislike the prospect of peace, even as other Syrians, notably those with business interests, develop expectations that go far beyond relations with Israel (for details on both camps, see Appendix III). Whether for or against, both sides seem to agree that a treaty with Israel represents much more than ending neighborly quarrel. Rather, they see it as a profound shift in the nature of their state. For the winners in today's Syria, a treaty threatens a way of life. For those seeking change, it represents an exit from totalitarian rule, with its repressions, poverty, and isolation, and a move into the American camp. As a young professor at Damascus University puts it, "We will expect democracy if peace comes."[3]

Assad probably fears that an agreement with Israel requiring "full peace" and normalization of relations will cause him to lose control, just as his Eastern European colleagues did during the Gorbachev era. How will he limit the pressures for economic equity, freedom of speech, improvements in human rights, ties to the outside world, and even meaningful elections? For someone who always relied on the *mukhabarat* state, the prospect of greater openness, more democracy, and even flocks of Israeli tourists in the *souks* of Damascus and Aleppo must be frightening. Assad presumably fears that such changes would endanger the position of his family and of the Alawi community.

If he does not in fact seek peace with Israel, why then does the Syrian president pursue negotiations with Israel in an apparently serious manner? As a way to improve his standing in Washington. To Syria, the point of the peace process is not to improve relations with Jerusalem but with Washington; in other words, Assad sees America as the new centerpiece of Syrian foreign policy.

---

[1] In particular, Peres could take the forthcoming statements he made as foreign minister ("The Golan Heights is Syrian land, and we are sitting on the Syrians' land," accepting the 1923 line as the Syrian-Israeli border) and formally re-issue them as government policy.

[2] The Cypriot foreign minister heard this from the Lebanese foreign minister, who had just returned from a meeting with Assad (*Ma'ariv*, March 21, 1995).

[3] *Los Angeles Times*, November 7, 1994.

Though peace itself may spell little but trouble, the peace process brings him many benefits; accordingly, his goal is not peace but a peace process. In short, Assad may have decided to participate in negotiations without intending for them to reach fruition. Engaging in apparently serious talks wins him improved relations with the West without having to open up his country. He can wink at the West while maintaining ties to Iran and hosting a wide range of terrorist groups.

This approach worked best when the Likud was in power, for Shamir's government could be relied on to maintain a hard line. Matters became more complicated when Rabin took over and made the historic decision to return virtually all the Golan Heights; Peres's flexibility puts even more pressure on Assad to take yes for an answer. Faced with such evident seriousness and good will, Assad has had to fall back on stalling tactics. Understanding his disinterest in a resolution with Israel helps clear up various mysteries, such as why in the twelve months after December 1994 Assad kept his negotiators from meeting their Israeli counterparts except for one formal round of talks; why he refuses unambiguously to signal his good intentions to the Israeli population; and why he says he sees no difference between the Rabin proposals for peace and those of the Likud party.

> We do not have a historical conflict with the Americans. Our only disagreement with them is their bias toward Israel.
>
> — Muhammad Salman, Syrian information minister[1]

> [Americans are] too honest to deal with Orientals.
>
> — Robert de Caix, a French imperial official, 1919[2]

A dilemma lies at the core of U.S. (and Western) policy toward Syria: what mixture of carrots and sticks is the best way to induce the country's crafty but imperiled leader to take steps that will make the Middle East a less volatile region? In good part, the answer to this question follows from a determination of Washington's top priority with regard to Syria. Is it most important to bring Hafez al-Assad into formal peaceful relations with Israel, no matter how cold and brittle that peace might be? Or is it getting Damascus to end its support for terrorism, its strategic alignment with Iran, its occupation of Lebanon, and its aggression against Turkey—even without an Israeli flag flying in Damascus?

More in Sorrow Than in Anger

Americans have plenty of reasons to be angry about the Assad regime's record. Not only was it for many years a voluntary member of the Soviet bloc and a strident opponent of U.S. foreign policy, but it has been complicit in the death of more Americans than any other government since the end of the Vietnam War. Damascus is probably responsible for the deaths of over four hundred Americans through its support for the 1983 bombing of a U.S. Marine barracks in Beirut, killing 241, and its likely role in the 1988 bombing of Pan Am 103 in

---

[1] *Al-Dustur* (Amman), November 23, 1992.

[2] Albert Howe Lybyer, "Diary," April 12, 1919, quoted in Harry N. Howard, *The King-Crane Commission: An American Inquiry in the Middle East* (Beirut: Khayat's, 1963), 45.

which 270 died, 175 of them American. It was also complicit in the seizure of over two dozen Americans in Lebanon, and continues to profit from the smuggling of drugs into the United States, the counterfeiting of U.S. currency, and the harboring of Nazi war criminals.[1]

Lesser problems also intrude. For example, Syrian pressure on the American medical supply company Baxter International led to the breaking of U.S. laws. On March 25, 1993, Baxter became the first-ever American company to plead guilty to a criminal charge connected with violating the U.S. anti-boycott legislation, admitting to having funneled $2 million in "fees" to Syrians in an attempt to have the company removed from the Arab boycott blacklist.[2]

This egregious behavior has not caused Washington to view Syria in the way it sees Libya, Iraq, and Iran, as a regime that needs to be isolated, weakened, and eventually changed. To the contrary, since December 1983, when the U.S. Navy lost two jets in a skirmish with Syrian forces over Lebanon, the U.S. government has pursued a more-in-sorrow-than-in-anger policy toward Damascus. Unlike Qadhafi and Saddam, seen as beyond hope, Assad appears to American policymakers as someone who can be redeemed, primarily by making peace with Israel.

These dissimilar hopes have large implications. While American leaders seek to break Libya, Iraq, and Iran—shunning them diplomatically, subjecting them to United Nations sanctions, and hitting them with American military force—Syria suffers no such indignities. Rather, U.S. politicians meet with their Syrian counterparts, discreetly raising objections in private and wooing them to become respectable and join the "family of nations." Four U.S. presidents have on five occasions met Assad (twice in Damascus, thrice in Geneva) and have spoken with him by telephone uncounted times. Secretaries of state make Damascus one of their most routine international stops;[3] Warren Christopher has visited Syria more often than any other foreign country—and as often as Britain, France, and Germany combined. In the other direction, Syria's foreign minister and chief of staff have the privilege of visiting the American capital (with the latter twice getting his picture taken with the president of the United States). Some exceedingly dubious figures connected with Syrian intelligence have also turned up in Washington, including

---

[1]   House Resolution 55, introduced on January 27, 1993, called on President Clinton to urge the Syrian authorities to extradite Aloïs Brunner.

[2]   *Wall Street Journal*, March 25 and 26, 1993; see also *New York Times*, March 26, 1993.

[3]   Henry Kissinger went there forty-one times in the course of his shuttle diplomacy and James A. Baker III stopped by on eight occasions in 1991 alone. In his first twenty-nine months in office, Warren Christopher visited Syria on thirteen different trips to the Middle East (and five times returned for a second stop on a trip, making eighteen times in all).

Brigadier General Ghazi Kan'an, the effective Syrian proconsul in Lebanon; Haydar Yusif, a suspected drug trafficker; and Munzir Qassar, an arms dealer subsequently arrested in Spain on grounds of "international terrorism,"[1] namely, smuggling explosives.

To encourage Assad, Washington makes exceptions to its own rules. Although U.S. law prohibits any equipment that can be used in war from going to Syria, the Bush administration decided after the Kuwait War to permit the Saudis to let Syrian troops take home some U.S.-made armored vehicles. In similar fashion, the Clinton administration permitted Kuwait to donate to Syria three used Boeing 727s in December 1993. A few months later, it delayed issuing the statutory report on terrorism by a month because Secretary Christopher was in the Middle East and the report would have embarrassed the Syrian leadership. In addition, the U.S. government even provides some aid to Syria. This not only includes a portion of the annual U.S. contribution to the Palestinian refugee relief agency, UNRWA,[2] but also country-to-country programs, like Fulbright exchange awards (which permit Syrians to study in the United States and Americans to study and teach in Syria) and funds for Syrian government officials and professionals to visit the United States.

U.S. officials hope that downplaying Assad's trespasses will create a friendly atmosphere and induce him to improve his behavior. For example, when other rogue states acquire ballistic missiles, alarm bells go off in Washington; in contrast, Syria's acquisition of such weapons was portrayed as having only a "defensive" purpose.[3] With regard to the Israel-PLO agreement, while Rabin noted that "although Syria is not directly involved in acts of aggression against Israel, it has made it possible for [the anti-DOP Palestinian organizations] to act,"[4] the U.S. government has adopted a more nuanced stance. While Assistant Secretary of State Robert H. Pelletreau at one point commended Assad for having "taken no steps to disrupt the growing Palestinian and Jordanian coexistence with Israel,"[5] other officials—including Christopher—have had cross words with their Syrian counterparts about Damascus's hospitality to those Palestinian rejectionist groups. In all, Washington has not permitted its pique to get in the way of the peace negotiations.

---

[1] *Le Monde,* June 6, 1992. Qassar was acquitted of the charges in Spain. See Manfred Morstein, *Der Tote des Terrors* (Munich: Piper, 1989).

[2] In May 1994, for example, the State Department announced an award of several million dollars for a new health center to pay for Palestinians in a Homs camp and a workshop in Damascus to provide Palestinians with job training (Reuters, May 12, 1994). In a totalitarian state such as Syria, no matter which agency receives outside money, the funds end up at the disposal of the government.

[3] *New York Times,* July 29, 1992.

[4] *Al-Ahram,* April 17, 1994.

[5] *U.S. Department of State Dispatch,* September 26, 1994.

American responses to Syrian terrorism best exemplify this reluctance to get tough with Damascus. For over ten years, American officials have chosen to recognize only some aspects of Syrian terrorism and waved away others. In one startling example, U.S. counterterrorism experts met with Syrian officials in July 1991 "in an effort to narrow differences on the terrorism issue." Some months later, the United States Information Agency paid for six Syrian security officials, including two senior military officers, to visit in the United States; in the course of their visit, they made orientation visits to the Drug Enforcement Administration;[1] that's like inviting foxes into chicken coop protection classes. Rejecting much evidence to the contrary—and especially *prima facie* evidence about Syria's role in Lebanon—the State Department maintains that "There is no evidence that Syrian officials have been directly involved in planning or executing terrorist attacks since 1986."[2] Illustrative of this attitude, Secretary of State James Baker refused in September 1991 to recognize Syrian support for the Turkish group Dev-Sol (See Appendix IV).

The outstanding example of this approach concerns the bombing of Pan Am 103 over Lockerbie in December 1988, killing 270. The U.S. government apparently decided to downplay Damascus's role, despite Syrian complicity in Ahmad Jibril's original planning of the operation. American officials did so by focusing on the narrow question of who built and planted the bomb, ignoring the earlier dimensions of conceptualizing and planning this operation. As investigative journalist Steven Emerson explains, the operation had three parts: "Iranians commissioned it, the Syrian-backed PFLP-GC planned the first attempt which didn't work, and handed off the operation to the Libyans, who actually carried it out."[3] When the operation is viewed in its totality, Syrian involvement in preparing the bombing, if not the bomb, is virtually indisputable. This evidence explains why Eliyahu Ben-Elissar, former chairman of the Israeli parliament's Foreign Affairs and Defense Committee, has flatly stated that "the Syrians and Jibril were involved in the Pan Am bombing."[4] In contrast, focusing only on the

---

[1]   Alfred B. Prados, "Syrian-U.S. Relations," a Congressional Research Service Issue Brief 92075 updated to October 7, 1994, 7, 14.

[2]   Department of State, *Patterns of Global Terrorism, 1994* (Washington, DC: Department of State Publication, 1995), 23. For ample evidence to the contrary, see Steven Emerson, "Is Syria Still Supporting Terrorism?" *Washington Post,* January 26, 1992.

[3]   Telephone interview, October 2, 1994. Indeed, the possibility that Damascus took part in the actual bombing has come to light. The BBC reported ("Silence Over Lockerbie," December 22, 1993) that Swiss timers thought sold only to Libya also went to the Stasi, the East German intelligence service with close ties to Damascus. Less credibly, another British documentary, "The Maltese Double Cross"—funded by Metropole Hotels, a company partially owned by the Libyan government—contended that a Syrian secret service officer made the bomb and a drug-trafficker named Khalid Ja'far carried the suitcase onto the flight under the impression he was carrying drugs.

[4]   IDF Radio, April 19, 1992.

third aspect of the operation appears to absolve Damascus—precisely what President Bush did when he dismissed any discussion of Syrian culpability as a "bum rap."[1]

The Syrians note the inconsistency of American policy. Minister of Information Muhammad Salman pointedly asks: "How can it be believed that Syria is a terrorist state when the U.S. president meets with President Assad, when the United States has an embassy in Damascus, and when the U.S. secretary of state has come to Syria scores of times?"[2]

How does Syria elude treatment as harsh as that meted out to other rogue states? In large part, by having a leader smarter than his counterparts in Libya, Iraq, and Iran. Appropriate and well-timed gestures by Assad encourage American leaders into thinking he can be shown the error of his ways (for example, with regard to terrorism). Cooperation on a host of lesser but emotional issues—getting American hostages out of Lebanon or Jews out of Syria—provides additional reasons for American officials to work with Damascus.

Most important of all, Assad has found one strategic reason after another to convince the U.S. government to treat him gently. Until August 1990, he enjoyed the protective shield of Soviet power. Then, as the Soviet threat lost its bite, Assad hopped sides and joined the anti-Iraq coalition; providing political cover for the alliance which protected him from August 1990 until March 1991. In the short but important period of March-July 1991, he made himself available to be wooed into the peace process. Since July 1991, he had to be humored for reasons related to negotiations with Jerusalem, one moment to stay in, another to participate constructively.

The decision to enter negotiations with Israel brings Assad two main benefits. First, it serves as a shield against criticism of all sorts. When Clinton's national security advisor, Anthony Lake, listed five "backlash" states, he included North Korea, Cuba, Iran, Iraq, and Libya but not Syria.[3] Asked about this omission, Lake replied that he specifically left Damascus off the list because of its participation in the peace process. While conceding that "there are certain similarities" between Syria and those other states, James Baker also placed Syria in a separate category, and for the same reason.[4] As Senator John Kerry prepared to hold hearings about Syrian drug trafficking in mid-1992, urgent requests to hold off came pouring in from—of all places—Jewish groups, especially the Council for the Rescue of Syrian Jews.

---

[1]   Associated Press, November 15, 1991.

[2]   *Al-Ahram*, December 10, 1992.

[3]   Anthony Lake, "Confronting Backlash States," *Foreign Affairs* (March/April 1994): 45-55. Sudan is another promising candidate for "backlash" status.

[4]   James A. Baker, III, "Looking Back on the Middle East," *Middle East Quarterly* (September 1994): 85. Baker also pointed to Syria's participation in the anti-Iraq coalition.

They reasoned that the hearings would delay the release of Syrian Jews, promised a few weeks earlier. In response, Kerry canceled the hearings. (As it turned out, exit visas for the Syrian Jews were delayed anyway for another year and a half.) When Ankara protested Syrian support of PKK terrorism in late 1993, the Syrians replied with seeming surprise, a London-based Arabic newspaper reported, "that this issue should be stirred up at a time when endeavors are being made to push the Middle East peace process forward between Syria and Israel."[1]

Second, talking to Israel assures Assad of virtual freedom of action in some other spheres. Take Lebanon: the U.S. government responded mildly to Assad's virtual annexation of that country in May 1991, out of fear that criticizing him would obstruct the peace process. The State Department did no more than warn Damascus that it expected Syrian troops to be withdrawn from parts of Lebanon in September 1992, as stipulated by the Ta'if accords. When the date came and went, neither the Bush nor the Clinton administration insisted on a Syrian pullback, wanting nothing to obstruct the peace process. For Assad, the peace process has many uses beyond its ostensible purpose.

A New Policy

For twelve years, Washington has pursued a highly nuanced policy. While Syria is on the list of terrorist-sponsoring and drug-trafficking states, Damascus escapes blame for many of its most reprehensible acts (hostage-taking in Lebanon, Pan Am 103). Though U.S. law prohibits many transactions with Syria (for details, see Appendix V), Assad wins a visit in Damascus from the president of the United States.

This subtle policy can claim some successes. Assad has bleached the Syrian stance of its old-style anti-Americanism and stopped terrorism against Westerners. He lent his considerable political weight to the allied effort in the Kuwait War. He agreed to negotiations with Israel. Syrian behavior in Lebanon improved. But key problems remain in place: Assad rules with totalitarian ruthlessness at home, mitigated only by some reversible improvements; and he engages in a host of aggressive policies abroad, building up an aggressive, offensive arsenal, maintaining at least some of the traditional hostility to Israel, and engaging in a wide variety of rogue activities. He has failed to live up to the "red line" understanding with Israel, two protocols signed with Turkey, and three agreements to leave Lebanon.

Is this mixed record the best the U.S. government can achieve or might a more assertive policy produce better results? The theme of this book is that the existing policy can be improved on, especially at this time of American strength and Syrian weakness. The time has come to look at Damascus in a new way.

---

[1]   *Al-Sharq al-Awsat*, November 3, 1993.

Undermine the Assad regime? Beginning with basics, Washington has a choice: to undermine the Assad regime or to improve it. For years, this author saw Assad as Syria's worst possible ruler from both the Syrian and American viewpoints, and so favored steps that would lead to a change in regime. Writing in 1990, for instance, I recommended that Americans should aim "to reduce [Assad's] capabilities or, better yet, to terminate his rule." I encouraged cooperation with the fundamentalist Muslims of Syria in the expectation that "gains derived from helping the Muslim Brethren [gain power] would outweigh the dangers."[1]

But times have changed. Two major developments turned international politics in the Middle East on their head: the leftist threat has largely abated with the collapse of the Soviet bloc, while fundamentalist Islam has become the region's greatest problem. As regards their threat to U.S. interests, right and left have changed places practically overnight. This reversal has profound implications for American policy. The top priority is no longer fending off the old aggressive, authoritarian alliance (of Marxist-Leninists) but fending off the new one (of fundamentalist Muslims). In days past, when faced with hostile left-wing regimes, Washington found allies in right-wing regimes ("friendly tyrants"). This made good sense, for while the leftists posed a serious threat to U.S. interests, the rightists did not. Roles having reversed, when faced with hostile fundamentalists, the U.S. government should now work with the isolated and less threatening left-wing regimes.

With regard to Assad, these global changes have transformed him from a leading figure in the Soviet alliance to someone who can potentially help resist the surge of fundamentalism. Recent developments, in short, have made Assad less of an opponent and more of an ally. Hüsamettin Çindoruk, speaker of the Turkish parliament, captured this point when he observed about the states ruled by Assad and Saddam Hussein that "We must endeavor to tolerate those regimes. Otherwise, we face fundamentalist regimes. Is that better?"[2]

Of course, Assad is not in every way a foe of fundamentalist Islam. He is an important, long-term ally of Iran, he helps sponsor Hezbollah in Lebanon, cooperates with Islamic Jihad in the West Bank and Gaza Strip, and has invited Hamas to make its headquarters in Damascus. If things went awry, he conceivably could follow Saddam Hussein's example and wrap himself in the green flag of fundamentalist Islam. But for the moment Assad stands resolutely against fundamentalist rule in Syria.

---

[1]   Daniel Pipes, "Comment contrer le 'Brejnev Syrien'?" *Politique Internationale* (Summer 1990): 167, 172.

[2]   *New York Times,* June 19, 1994.

There is another reason why it is probably best for Assad to stay. The widespread decay of totalitarian states in the past five years teaches that a slow, controlled transition works better than a rapid one, especially where ethnic and ideological conflict are likely. It appears easier to attain prosperity and national power than the rule of law and personal freedom. The Polish model, in other words, works better than the Yugoslav one. Applied to Syria, this conclusion suggests that Assad could play a key role in avoiding a Sunni-Alawi fratricidal war.

Improve the Assad regime. For these reasons, the distasteful conclusion is that it is currently in America's interest for Assad to remain in power. Therefore, U.S. policy should aim to "improve" rather than undermine his rule—improvements most likely evident in limited shifts, not fundamental changes.

First, outside powers should concentrate on foreign, not domestic, policy. Governments do not normally allow pressure from abroad to undercut their authority at home (a point starkly confirmed by arguments over Most Favored Nation status with the People's Republic of China). Syrian foreign policy is both what the U.S. government most objects to and what Assad can afford to most readily change.

Second, improving the regime does not imply that Assad becomes an American ally. Some analysts actually see this move as already made;[1] others expect Assad to make this leap like Anwar al-Sadat, who moved himself and his country from the Soviet camp to the American one. They are likely to be disappointed. Sadat gloried in the large and dramatic gesture, and left the details for aides to work on; in contrast, Assad is a famously parsimonious negotiator who revels in specifics and never gives anything away. At best, he fulfills the letter of his agreements (and often much less);[2] to imagine him getting carried away with the spirit of the agreement completely misjudges the man.

With Assad, the peace process is the key to little beyond itself. Negotiations with Israel will not carry other issues such as relations with Iran or support for terrorism. (In this respect, Assad will be more like Yasser Arafat.) Should the U.S. government truly seek a Sadat-like shift from one camp and way of ruling to another, it must demand just that. Given America's leverage over Syria, this is the moment to press Assad to opt for a coherent, Western-oriented course. And that requires a far greater readiness to confront Damascus than has been the case since early 1984. This suggests the need for a two-pronged course of action, starting with the peace process and building to an ambitious program to transform Syria.

---

[1]   Patrick Seale says that Syria "has virtually switched camps from East to West." See his preface in Eberhard Kienle, ed., *Contemporary Syria: Liberalization Between Cold War and Cold Peace* (New York: St. Martin's Press, 1994), ix.

[2]   Despite his reputation for scrupulously fulfilling obligations, Assad has in fact a dubious record on this score. For details, see the author's analysis in "Does Assad Keep His Word?" *Jerusalem Post*, August 19, 1994.

Peace process. Step One involves winning improvements in the single most critical issue from an American point of view—relations with Israel. U.S. officials should accept Syrian improvements *vis-à-vis* Israel, reward Assad in small ways for these, then demand more. If he offers nothing more, they should continue to work with him on a limited basis, all the while pressuring him for more. A breakthrough here justifies an improvement in U.S.-Syrian relations, not an alliance. No matter how useful his foreign policy, so long as Assad runs a totalitarian state at home with expansionist designs abroad, he cannot enjoy close U.S. government association or support. Specifically, this means no public money in aid (business investments, however, are acceptable). The American public cannot sustain alliances with dictators, as failed efforts with Muhammad Reza Pahlavi, Ferdinand Marcos, and many others proved. Nor should it: the Syrian public might well remember any U.S. support for Assad long after he and his henchmen are gone, and that anger could hurt U.S. interests in the long-term. While peace with Israel would improve the two states' relations, a treaty alone would leave the two parties mistrustful and chilly (as, for example, Israel and the PLO have remained since September 1993).

Transformation. Step Two means achieving a progressive shift in policy, so that Assad does most of what the West wants of him. This means a warm peace with Israel, a withdrawal from Lebanon, an ending of the PKK insurgency against Turkey, and no mischief in Iraq. With time, it should also mean a modest opening within Syria, including autonomous economic institutions and some personal freedoms. Should the Syrian regime truly undergo so radical a change of behavior, it can claim substantial rewards from the West. As in the case of other prodigal leaders (e.g. Sadat, Mikhail Gorbachev), Assad should gain access to the West's economic strength and possibly even to its arsenal. The possibility then exists for cooperation on a range of questions, including fundamentalist Islam, Iraq, and water issues.

Assad can help by staving off fundamentalist Muslim elements in Syria and keeping them out of power in his own country; beyond that, he can take a number of steps useful to U.S. interests. After having broken with his fundamentalist friends and clients—the Iranian regime, Hezbollah, Hamas, and Islamic Jihad—Assad should be encouraged to take the lead in maintaining a political alternative to fundamentalist rule. In this regard, he has something novel to offer his neighbors: the Association of Islamic Charitable Projects (*Jam'iyat Mashari' al-Islamiya al-Khayriya*), a Sunni religious organization apparently sponsored by Damascus with growing international reach. Based on the ideas of 'Abdullah al-Harari, an Ethiopian thinker, the AICP provides services similar to the fundamentalist organizations (e.g., health clinics) while promoting a staunchly anti-fundamentalist outlook.

The Syrian government already has a number of constructive positions on Iraq. It sides more with the coalition than with Baghdad whenever confrontation looms. It works with the Turkish and Iranian governments to maintain Iraqi territorial integrity. Looking to the future, it would help greatly if Syria would cease supporting its own clique of anti-Saddamists in Damascus and instead help develop a constructive Middle East diplomacy toward Baghdad. This would mean supporting the Iraqi National Congress (a collection of ethnic and ideological groups) or some other responsible organization.

While a good part of the Levant's current water problems could be resolved if market mechanisms—not political whims—governed the distribution of water, the region will need new hydraulic supplies if it is to continue producing agricultural goods. And those supplies realistically can come from only one source—Turkey. Turkish leaders have from time to time raised the subject of exporting water to the Levant and even to the Arabian peninsula, but as Israel's Rabin noted, "there is nothing to be done as long as a peace agreement is not signed with Syria and Lebanon."[1] Once this occurs, the possibility of massive water works comes into existence.

Premises of a new approach. Such dramatic improvements in the Assad regime are not likely to take place so long as Washington pursues the accommodating policy of recent years. They become more likely if the U.S. government adopts an approach to Damascus simultaneously more diffident and tougher, one that while closely involved with the peace process looks beyond Syrian negotiations with Israel and tracks more closely with American policies toward pariah states. Important premises of such a policy include:

See Syria as a whole. U.S. officials should view Syria through something larger than the Israeli prism. However important, the peace process is not the be-all of U.S. interests in Syria and should not obscure other important issues concerning Syria. The occupation of Lebanon, the destabilization of Turkey, the bombing of Pan Am 103 and other terrorist attacks, the military buildup, and drug trafficking are important in their own right.

Become less eager. Remember that Assad needs the West far more than the West needs him. Rather than win Syrian favor, sit back and let him seek out Washington. Do not signal a need for Syria to achieve a more stable and prosperous Middle East but let Syria suffer from economic malaise and political isolation. Assad needs to worry about the United States, not the reverse.

Get tougher. An authoritarian leader such as Assad responds to pressure, not goodwill gestures. When Assad engages in activities contrary to American interests, he needs to hear about it. Respond to his positive actions with less delight and more equanimity: "Thank you;

---

[1]   TRT Television (Ankara), November 2, 1994.

what will you give us next?" Eliminate the little concessions Assad takes as his due and does not reciprocate. When presenting a plan to Congress to waive U.S. regulations and permit Kuwait to transfer three Boeing planes to Syria, for example, State Department officials implied this concession was critical to bringing Damascus back into the negotiating process. In fact, upon learning about the U.S. decision to permit the transfer, the Syrian foreign minister "showed no appreciation" but "regarded it as a virtually meaningless gesture."[1]

Push for a commitment. Ze'ev Schiff writes that Damascus "must decide whether to return to the 1974 model of preparing itself to stand alone against Israel or to take the Egyptian (and Saudi) path of seeking a diplomatic solution;"[2] Assad's biography makes clear that he commits only when necessary and otherwise keeps all options open, holding out for better breaks down the road. Schiff is right that the West must push Assad into making this stark choice—but the choice goes beyond Syrian policy toward Israel. It boils down to "You're either with us or against us." He can work with the West or enter on a collision course with it; make basic changes or stick with the policies of the last quarter century. Will he work with the United States and its allies, or with the Islamic Republic of Iran and its epigones? The choice, Assad must be made to understand, is his, and he cannot evade it.

Draw a dark picture of the anti-American route. Assad needs to be told in no uncertain terms that the alternative to cooperation is ending up like Saddam, Kim Jong Il, or Castro—isolated, weak, and losing ground. In other words, he and the Alawi people have no viable alternative to the Western route.

Assad's likely choice. Which route will Assad choose? Both are problematic. The American route requires him to abandon one of the two mainstays of a quarter-century's rule, aggressiveness abroad (the other is repression at home), and so to give up old habits, old allies, and successful policies without any guarantees that the new ones will serve him better. The Iranian route threatens to isolate Assad internationally, and so weaken his rule domestically.

Not being in crisis, why should Assad go the American route, putting aside the habits of a lifetime and taking terrible risks? Because it promises a better future for him and the Alawi people. The West has much that Assad wants: economic aid, investments, and trade; enormous influence over Turkey and Israel; and the currency of legitimacy. Fear of the United States—especially the larger-than-life would-be hegemony imagined in Damascus—also prompts Assad to accommodate.

---

[1] *Forward,* December 17, 1993; see also *New York Times,* December 7, 1993.

[2] Ze'ev Schiff, *Peace With Security: Israel's Minimal Security Requirements in Negotiations with Syria,* Policy Paper Number Thirty-Four (Washington, DC: The Washington Institute for Near East Policy, 1993), 73. Schiff himself notes that "Assad has decided to go along two different routes at the same time—political and military."

In the end, Assad probably will decide that while the Iranian route pleases him, the American one serves him better. Rephrasing the choice in his own terms, the American route better assures him and his coreligionists, the Alawis, continued domination of Syrian politics. As a canny and disciplined pragmatist, he will do what he has to do, however distasteful it may be, even if that means acquiescing to Western demands. If necessity requires him to make a deal with the United States, or even with Israel, he will do so (and deliver a long speech on how this is consistent with the last quarter-century's struggle). The record of recent years points in this direction. Assad has already moved toward the West in an attempt to free himself from the limited sanctions against him and to create a partnership with the Cold War's victors. He has made significant changes; he would probably make more, if only he felt he had to. That's where a well-designed American policy can make a difference.

Policy Recommendations

Getting down to specifics, the Executive Branch can pressure Damascus in a variety of ways, using psychology, diplomacy, and bilateral relations. In addition, Congress has an important role to play.

Most of the world has learned three things about the United States since 1991. First, Americans have no intention of taking advantage of their victory in the Cold War to dominate other countries, as evidenced by the steep drop in funding for the defense budget. Second, the "New World Order" was a banal, dimly conceived notion that had completely disappeared well before George Bush lost the presidency. Third, the Clinton administration wishes the rest of the world to leave it alone so it can concentrate on domestic issues.

These realities have not, for the most part, reached the Middle East. To the contrary, Arab and Iranian leaders vastly exaggerate American will, insisting that Washington plans to rule the globe (this appears to be projection; they assume Americans are doing what they would do in the cat seat). A Damascus newspaper states, for example, that a World War III will continue until "every U.S. ministry becomes a ministry of the whole world."[1] The New World Order constitutes a fearsome and existing reality to many in the Middle East, and is regularly railed against by leaders and media. Middle Easterners even filter failed U.S. engagements (e.g., Somalia, Bosnia) through their conspiratorial imaginations and reinterpret them to come out in the U.S. favor. They distort American goals (the troops went to Somalia to battle Islam) or turn apparent defeats into devious victories (in Bosnia, for example, Washington succeeded to destroy a new Muslim country in Europe). American declaratory statements in themselves, without plans to follow them up operationally, are likely to have a powerful

---

[1]   *Al-Ba'th,* June 22, 1992.

impact on Assad. He is one leader still impressed by the White House bully pulpit.

With imagination, the U.S. government can take advantage of these distortions to gain leverage over leaders like Hafez al-Assad. His fears render him more likely to appease Washington than to confront it. A U.S. diplomacy more angry and less sorrowful has a good chance of substantially influencing Syrian behavior. For example, official Syria shows continued distress at being listed on the terrorism and drug trafficking lists; this hints at the potential impact of severe criticism. Should Washington condemn Assad's many other trespasses this would likely change the calculus of decisionmaking in Damascus.

Of all these statements, probably the most important is a strong, unequivocal condemnation of continued Syrian control of Lebanon, for the U.S. government has not yet, in almost twenty years, gone on the record opposing that occupation. As cases from around the world show (communist control of China, Soviet control of the Baltic states, Israeli control of East Jerusalem), merely for Washington to assert a principle of non-recognition can have a great impact on the course of events.

But Washington's efforts should go beyond the merely declaratory to include three diplomatic initiatives. First, should high-level American officials (more or less indiscreetly) help Ankara and Jerusalem coordinate their policies *vis-à-vis* Syria, some beneficial shudders would no doubt shake the halls of power in Damascus. The basis of this Turkish-Israeli cooperation has already been laid. The two states began negotiating a free trade agreement in early 1993. On a visit to Israel in November 1993, then-Foreign Minister Çetin broke a paramount Middle East taboo and signed a Strategic Cooperation Agreement with Israel. Two of its five accords concern the exchange of military technology and cooperating to prevent disputes. Over the next year, the two states signed agreements to combat terrorism, drug trafficking, and organized crime. They also reached an agreement, along with the U.S. government, to work together on agricultural projects in Central Asia. Prime Minister Tansu Çiller announced her public readiness to work with Israel in the war against Hezbollah terrorism.[1] Her trip to Israel in November 1994—the first for a Turkish prime minister—then did much generally to enhance the two states' ties.

Damascus must have taken particular note of the agreement signed to cooperate against terrorism and drug trafficking, the dramatic summoning to Israel by Çiller of her intelligence advisor (who flew in on a special plane), and a deal (now formalized) by which Israeli technicians modernize Turkey's F-4 fighter jets. Reports of a joint guided missile project could set off even louder alarm bells in

---

[1] *Yedi'ot Ahronot,* January 28, 1994.

Damascus. And late-Prime Minister Rabin's suggestion about bringing Egypt into a three-way pact to repress terrorism might open the way to a cooperation even more ominous to Damascus. All these steps fuel Syrian apprehensions, leading to unfounded worries of more Turkish-Israeli collaboration than actually is the case.[1]

Second, Washington should signal its growing impatience for Assad to reach a deal with Israel. Steps could include: increasing support for Israeli positions in the peace negotiations; signals that Israel has Washington's blessing for forceful retaliation against terrorist groups operating in Lebanon; and joint exercises with Israeli forces in the Levantine waters or in the Galilee.

Third, the United States can focus on specific, bilateral pressures. Being listed as a terrorist-sponsoring state deprives Syria from acquiring American arms, "dual-use" technology—that is, civilian equipment that can be used for military purposes—or financial assistance. The additional sanctions imposed on Syria in November 1986 (by way of punishment for official Syrian complicity in the attempted bombing of an El Al airplane) limit sales of such items as helicopters and aircraft, ban Export-Import Bank credits, block loans from the International Monetary Fund and World Bank, and terminate an aviation agreement. In the name of the peace process, however, such restrictions have periodically been overridden by executive waiver. These exceptions should cease.

American firms operate in Syria almost without restrictions; further limitation on commercial ties would cause consternation in Damascus. Not only do the authorities seek more foreign investment but American technology has particular importance in the petroleum industry. Without it, Syrian production may soon go into decline.[2]

Unfortunately, recent steps have gone in the opposite direction. The Office of Export Administration at the Department of Commerce slightly loosened its policy toward Syria in the aftermath of the Kuwait War and in anticipation of the Madrid peace process. Before September 1, 1991, a potential exporter had to prove to the office why he should be granted a license to send goods to Syria; this presumption of denial meant that a proposed sale got rejected unless a good reason existed for it to go through. Since that date the burden of proof has passed to the office. In similar fashion, Syria was on October 6, 1993

---

[1] For example, *al-Shira'*, a Lebanese news weekly that often reflects Syrian thinking, claimed in its issue of April 3, 1995 that "the most recent instance of coordination between Turkey and Israel is the presence of more than fifty Israeli military experts in Ankara to put Israel's experience in southern Lebanon to use in northern Iraq."

At the same time, Turkish and Israeli interests in an Israel-Syria peace may clash to the extent that a peace agreement between Syria and Israel could lead to the redeployment of Syrian troops against Turkey. According to one report (*Ma'ariv*, June 5, 1995), the Turks have already made themselves heard on this matter.

[2] *Energy Compass*, January 21, 1994.

removed from the list of "special countries" ineligible for materials which they can use (or trade to others) for building nuclear weapons.[1] Unless there is good reason to the contrary, these decisions need to be reversed.

Small amounts of U.S. taxpayer money go to a Syria, symbolically rewarding the Assad regime when it remains a rogue state. Until Damascus improves its behavior, it should receive no U.S. public funds at all. In addition, high-ranking officials should stop trading visits, and laws should be applied with fewer exceptions.

It is worth recalling—and reminding Syrian authorities—that the U.S. government has many ways to turn up the pressure on Assad should he revert to his ways of old. It could sponsor a Radio Free Syria. If U.S. forces do not already shadow vessels bringing materiel to Syria, they could begin to do so. They could also closely—and somewhat conspicuously—monitor Syrian military ships and planes. U.S. officials can send out feelers to the Assad regime's opponents. Were the secretary of state to meet with leaders of non-fundamentalist Sunni groups from Syria, the message would get through loud and clear; as would his chatting with a few anti-Syrian Maronite figures. (Plenty of precedents for such steps exist, including meetings with non-official Palestinians and Iraqis; but the South Africa example may be the most relevant, for meetings with the African National Congress leadership took place simultaneously with official diplomatic relations.) Washington could also consider providing support to the opposition movements.

Congress has an especially important role in relations with Syria. Not only does Damascus pay precise attention to statements coming out of Washington, but it also tends to see the Senate and House as less than autonomous bodies, so what Congress does will be understood as a signal coming from the White House (as is the case when the Syrian parliament makes a decision). When the Senate passed a non-binding resolution in March 1990 deeming Jerusalem the capital of Israel, hardly anyone noticed in the United States but politicians and media all over the Middle East, including Syria, became alarmed. Similarly, when Congress voted unanimously in July 1993 to assert that it "considers the Government of Syria in violation of the Ta'if agreement,"[2] the Assad regime took close note.

---

[1] There is at least one example of policy on Syria being tightened in recent years. Damascus long benefited from the General System of Preferences (GSP), a program which lets poor countries export manufactured goods to the United States with minimal tariffs. Although the GSP contains provisions requiring workers' rights and prohibiting terrorism, neither of which the Assad regime meets, AFL-CIO efforts to exclude Syria from 1988 on, citing Syrian failure to uphold Sections 502 and 504 of the U.S. Trade Act of 1974, met with failure. Only in 1992 did the Congress approve a Bush administration proposal to take away the Syrian privileges.

[2] U.S. Congress Concurrent Resolution 28, July 1, 1993. A second, weaker resolution

Congress can pressure the Executive branch to show some spine. Congress has at least two important functions in this regard. First, it can pressure the Executive branch and monitor its efforts. In 1994, for example, Republicans and Democrats worked together to play a critical role in assuring that government functionaries did not take Syria off the terrorism and narcotics lists. Second, Congress can close the "national interest" loopholes that permit the Executive branch to waive regulations, and which it seems to do disproportionately for Damascus. Instead, Congress can require its consent before regulations are relaxed.

The ultimate goal of making basic improvements in Assad's regime—decency at home, peaceable relations abroad—would make Syria effectively aligned with the United States. This remote but not impossible event would have important consequences not just for the fourteen million inhabitants of Syria but also for much of the Middle East. By giving up his bellicose policies abroad, Assad lowers the temperature throughout the Middle East. Syria's acceptance of the Jewish state would mean Israel no longer faces an existential threat from its neighbors. For Turkey, a breakthrough with Syria means a severe weakening of the PKK and a major boost in the country's security. For Lebanon, it means a chance at independence again. For the PLO, it means a better opportunity to prevail against rejectionist elements. For all, it would mean that the Middle East's roster of rogue states (Libya, Sudan, Iraq, Iran) loses a charter member and becomes correspondingly far less powerful. A transformation of Syria would tilt the Middle East balance of power further in the West's favor, much to the advantage of both the region and the West.

---

passed the House on June 7, 1995.

APPENDICES

APPENDIX I

THE ANTI-ARAFAT ALLIANCE

Eight leftist Palestinian groups opposed to the Israel-PLO Declaration of Principles base their operations in Syria or in Syrian-controlled Lebanon. They are (in alphabetical order, with founding dates in parenthesis):

* Democratic Front for the Liberation of Palestine (1969), a Maoist splinter of the PFLP led by Na'if Hawatma;
* Fatah al-Intifada (1983), a splinter of Fatah led by Sa'id Musa Muragha (known as Abu Musa);
* Palestine Liberation Front (1977), a splinter of the PFLP-GC with factions led by Muhammad 'Abbas and Tal'at Ya'qub;
* Palestinian Peoples' Party (1920s), formerly the Communist Party, led by Bashir Barghuti (lives in Jerusalem);
* Palestinian Popular Struggle Front (1968), a splinter of Fatah led by Samir Ghawsha;
* Popular Front for the Liberation of Palestine (1967), an intensely ideological group led by George Habash (and, as his health declines, increasingly run by Abu 'Ali Mustafa);
* Popular Front for the Liberation of Palestine-General Command (1968), a particularly violent splinter of the PFLP led by Ahmad Jibril;
* Al-Sa'iqa (1968-69), an arm of the Syrian government, led by 'Isam al-Qadi.

Two Palestinian organizations of a fundamentalist Islamic orientation also oppose the DOP and have facilities in Syrian-controlled territory:

* Hamas (1987), a pro-Iranian group, led by Ahmad Yasin; and
* Islamic Jihad (1980), a splinter of the Muslim Brethren formerly led by Fat'hi al-Shaqaqi and currently led by Ramadan Abdallah Shallah.

Soon after the Declaration of Principles was signed, these ten groups joined together to form a group variously known as the National, Democratic, and Islamic Front, the Alliance of Palestinian Forces, or the Palestinian Grouping. The Front's importance lies in its bringing together leftist and fundamentalist organizations to form a specifically anti-Arafat alliance.

Other rejectionist Palestinian groups also cooperate with these ten. The Fatah Revolutionary Council (1973), led by Abu Nidal, may be headquartered in Syria; it certainly has some presence there and works at times with the Syrian regime. The Iraqi-sponsored Arab Liberation Front (1969) withdrew its support from Arafat and may have started working with the Damascus-based groups.

<u>APPENDIX II</u>

SYRIAN-BACKED TERRORISM IN BERLIN

Until recently, official Syrian complicity in terrorism was mostly a matter of conjecture; with the exception of the Hindawi affair, when a British court convicted a Syrian agent of the crime, there was little hard evidence of Damascus's participation. But with the collapse of the East German state and the opening of the files belonging to its secret police, the Stasi, information is accumulating about Syrian activities abroad before 1989. The Stasi archives have proven very important, for example, in unraveling the 1983 bombing of West Berlin's French cultural center, the Maison de France.

The story began in mid-1983, when Johannes Weinrich brought 53 pounds of explosives into East Berlin. The Stasi discovered and confiscated these explosives and placed them in a depot controlled by Lt. Col. Helmut Voigt of Stasi's counterterrorism unit. Once Voigt ascertained that the explosive material was indeed to be used by Carlos, he transferred it to the Syrian embassy in East Berlin, where Nabil Charitah, the third secretary, accepted it; he stored the explosives in the office of Ambassador Faysal Summaq, then turned them over to Weinrich. Weinrich carried the bomb across the border to West Berlin and used it to blow up the Maison de France on August 25, 1983, killing one and wounding twenty-three. Summaq then brought Weinrich back to safety in East Berlin in his own limousine bearing diplomatic tags. In a letter to the West German embassy in Saudi Arabia, Carlos claimed responsibility for the explosion.

Charitah turned state's witness against Voigt and now lives under German police protection. In April 1994, Voigt was sentenced to four years in jail for his part in the bombing—the first Stasi agent imprisoned for crimes carried out in the course of his official duties. Summaq (deemed by one newspaper "the most important link between Arab terrorism and the eastern [European] secret services")[1] was arrested in Vienna in October 1994 on the grounds that during his eight years in East Berlin he planned and ordered a number of terrorist attacks, including the 1975 kidnapping of OPEC ministers in Vienna. Political pressures (and perhaps intimidation by Damascus)[2] led to his quick release, however, and he returned to Syria.[3]

---

[1] *Kurier* (Vienna), October 28, 1994.

[2] *Der Spiegel,* November 28, 1994.

[3] *Neue Kronen-Zeitung,* October 27 and November 7, 1994; see also *Wiener Zeitung,* November 29, 1994.

APPENDIX III

DO SYRIANS WANT PEACE WITH ISRAEL?

As the possibility of an agreement between Damascus and Jerusalem appears more likely, the question arises: What do Syrians think about their two-generation conflict with Israel? No reply can be given with confidence, it being next to impossible to study public opinion in a totalitarian state like Syria. Syrians on the street have learned to parrot the official line as expertly as cabinet ministers. A law school student acknowledges, "We can only have the same opinion as President Assad. Everything he says, I agree with." [1] Still, bits of evidence exist and it is worth making a try to bring them together, for this gives an important insight into the future of the Arab-Israeli conflict.

Know More

To begin with, for several years Syrians have been learning more about Israel. A country once portrayed as satanic has become less mythical and more normal. Already in 1990, an unnamed "senior member" of Assad's entourage told an Israeli reporter:

> It is much easier now. There are foreign papers; tourists arrive after a visit to Israel and we talk to them; television airs mostly films about the *intifada*, so you can imagine how you [Israelis] are portrayed in them. We also listen to your radio broadcasts, particularly the newsreels. Besides, those of us who should know things about you do. The "Israeli enemy" is a fact of life. [2]

This increase in information surely has the long-term effect of improving Syrian attitudes towards a democracy—a speculation confirmed by the small but steady number of Syrian military deserters finding their way to Israel.

End the Conflict

Other Syrians clearly want to end the conflict. Muhammad 'Aziz Shukri, dean of Damascus University's law school, told an American reporter in 1991: "There's a segment of the [Syrian] population that says, 'I'm not interested in the Arab-Israeli conflict. I just want a bottle of gas [for the kitchen stove].'" [3] Two years later, he ventured further: "Let us teach our kids that the Israelis are not animals, and let the

---

[1] *Jerusalem Report*, January 28, 1993.

[2] *Yedi'ot Ahronot*, July 20, 1990. Israeli leaders sense Syrian eyes on them; when he was chief of staff, Ehud Barak said, "The Syrians monitor every remark we make" (*al Hamishmar*, September 14, 1994).

[3] *Jerusalem Report*, December 12, 1991.

Israelis teach their kids that we are not animals. Up to now, unfortunately, our behavior is of animals in the zoo."[1] A thirty-year-old professional woman echoed his sentiments: "We want to stop hearing every day about Israeli aggression and start hearing about Syria."[2]

Interest in the Palestinian cause seems to have waned over the decades. Nabil 'Ali, a Damascene clerk, commented "Let's never mind the others. We should just get back the Golan and be finished with it."[3] Getting the Golan back comes up fairly often as a requirement for peace: Fadi, a civil engineer in his last year of school, says that "If Israel would just give it back, there would be no problem."[4]

Business Interests

Business interests show the greatest enthusiasm for ending the conflict. "People are tired," a merchant reports.[5] A businessman named Abu'l-Huda Lahham notes that while Assad makes the decisions of war and peace, "when the door is open, we'll be ready for business."[6] Walid, a dealer in embroidered tablecloths, told an Israel-based journalist to "Please tell the Israelis that we have very good prices here. We want them to come." His brother Faris added, "Peace will be good for Syria and Israel together." On leaving, Faris told the journalist, "Come back. Bring your friends from Jerusalem."[7] Travelers report that Damascene restaurants are preparing menus in Hebrew and that merchants in the market look forward to Israeli customers. Bassam al-Subayni, a Damascus shopkeeper, flatly says he wants peace with Israel because "Peace means more business."[8] Or, Muhammad 'Adnan, a taxi driver: "Soon, God willing, Damascus will be filled with more business people and tourists, even tourists from Israel."[9] In the same spirit, three tour operators defied the Ministry of Tourism and joined their Israeli counterparts at a tourism conference in Cairo in late 1994.

In an intriguing bit of business optimism, the price for land in the abandoned Syrian city of Qunaytra, right on the border with Israel, has roughly quadrupled between mid-1994 and mid-1995; some Syrian investors, it would seem, expect peace with Israel, thereby returning Qunaytra into a place for the living. Of course, these investors thereby have a vested interest in peace being established with Israel.

---

[1] *Wall Street Journal Europe*, January 14-15, 1994.

[2] *New York Times*, December 17, 1991.

[3] Ibid., September 21, 1993.

[4] *Christian Science Monitor*, August 22, 1994.

[5] Larry Cohler, "Rethinking Syria," *Tikkun*, September/October 1992, 32.

[6] *Washington Times*, August 17, 1994.

[7] *Jerusalem Report*, December 1, 1994.

[8] *New York Times*, October 28, 1994.

[9] Ibid., October 30, 1994.

Intensify the Conflict

But this is not the only view: others want to intensify the conflict. Four constituencies appear to lead the opposition to peace with Israel.

(1) Fundamentalist Muslims portray Assad as an Israeli agent and condemn the peace process as a betrayal. Although weak, they remain a latent force in Syrian politics.

(2) Intellectuals and professionals still warm themselves by the flame of Pan-Arab nationalism. Suhayl Zakkar, a professor of history at Damascus University, remarks that he has "learned two things as a Muslim in the past fifty years. There is one God, and there is one enemy, the Israeli." An unnamed female Syrian social researcher confirms this point: "You can have an authoritarian government like Assad's that can make anything stick. But popular acceptance of Israel is another story."[1] The Union of Syrian Writers froze the membership of Adonis, perhaps Syria's leading poet, for his favoring contacts "with the Zionist enemy."[2] Jamal al-Atassi, one of Syria's few dissidents, disapproves of recent developments and sees the government as a patsy: "The regime is just trying to do what the United States wants it to do."[3] The regime counters the influence of these naysayers by carrying out a campaign of persuasion in the schools and universities.

(3) Ba'th Party members, numbering a quarter-million or so, are described by the *Christian Science Monitor* as the "most opposed to peace."[4] In one intriguing insight, Argentine officials accompanying President Carlos Menem to Syria came away with the impression that Foreign Minister Faruq al-Sharaa "maintains tougher stands regarding Israel than does President Hafez al-Assad."[5]

(4) According to a Western diplomat in Damascus, "The strongest voice resisting peace right now comes from people in the military and security apparatus who have been making fortunes [from the confrontation with Israel]."[6] Special Russian envoy for Middle Eastern issues Viktor Posuvalyuk reportedly confided to the Israelis that he had found "substantial centers of opposition" to an agreement "at the highest echelons of the Syrian administration."[7] The Syrian chief of staff reportedly told his Israeli interlocutors about similar problems.[8]

At the same time, reports from Israel indicate that Assad is taking extraordinary steps to convince the military-security apparatus of his policies. He consulted with top military officers before taking part in

---

[1] *Christian Science Monitor*, October 20, 1993.

[2] *Al-Shira'*, February 6, 1995.

[3] Cohler, "Rethinking Syria," 30.

[4] *Christian Science Monitor*, September 20, 1994.

[5] *Ha'aretz*, December 15, 1994.

[6] *Los Angeles Times*, November 7, 1994.

[7] *Ma'ariv*, August 26, 1994.

[8] Kol Yisra'el, July 18, 1995.

the peace process negotiations; he polls them to ascertain their views on the prospect of peace with Israel; and he (and other top officials, such as Sharaa) holds occasional meetings with top commanders at which, according to an Israeli newspaper, he "preaches to them the need for peace" with Israel—suggesting that the military leadership is "not totally at ease with the idea."[1] This campaign seems to be working, for Israeli military intelligence says it "cannot identify any Syrian opposition that will disrupt" a decision to go forward with peace.[2]

Change Over Time

Survey research suggests that Syrian opinion is changing in favor of peaceable relations. A "modest commercial survey" in the fall of 1991 in Damascus found just 30 percent favoring the Madrid Conference.[3] Another 1991 poll showed supporters numbering about one-fifth of the population, while a July 1993 survey in Syria found 28 percent in support of peace talks.[4] Contrast these results with survey information from 1994: the support ranges from a low of 30 percent to 45 percent, a change Hilal Khashan of the American University of Beirut deems "very remarkable." Khashan concludes that "Assad's preparation of his people for peace appears to be paying off."[5]

Observers are divided on what this amounts to. Syrian poet Mamdu' 'Adwan believes that "The majority of Syrians disagree with the regime's domestic and human rights practices but agree with its foreign policy,"[6] even as it moderates toward Israel. Impressed by the peaceable mood in Damascus, journalist David Butter reported in October 1992 that "Syrians are overwhelmingly in favor of the moves towards peace with Israel."[7] Geoffrey Aronson agrees: "Open borders, even an Israeli Embassy in Damascus, pose little problem in the streets and offices of Damascus."[8] More cautiously, Jonathan Ferziger of the Associated Press concluded at the end of 1994 that, "among the people of his capital city at least, [Assad's] task of preparing Syrian public opinion for peace seems to be advancing apace."[9]

---

[1] *Yedi'ot Ahronot*, September 16, 1994; see also *Ha'aretz*, July 19, 1995.

[2] Uri Saguy, *Davar*, September 5, 1994.

[3] David Pollock, *The "Arab Street"? Public Opinion in the Arab World*, Policy Paper Number Thirty-Two (Washington, DC: The Washington Institute for Near East Policy, 1992), 53-54.

[4] Hilal Khashan, "Are the Arabs Ready for Peace with Israel?" *Middle East Quarterly* (March 1994): 21.

[5] Hilal Khashan, "The Levant: Yes to Treaties, No to Normalization," *Middle East Quarterly* (June 1995): 5.

[6] Cohler, "Rethinking Syria," 34.

[7] *Middle East Economic Digest*, October 9, 1992.

[8] Geoffrey Aronson, "Syria Now Sees, Reluctantly, Benefits of Peace with Israel," *Christian Science Monitor*, August 22, 1994.

[9] Jonathan Ferziger, "The Price is Right," *The Jerusalem Report*, December 1, 1994.

Who's Ahead: Populace or Regime?

Finally, the core question: Who is more prone to make peace with Israel, the populace or the regime? Assessments break down into two camps. Western diplomats in Damascus observe that "The people outside the regime are much more prepared for peace than the elites are"[1] and that the people "are ahead of the leadership."[2] As though confirming this point, unsigned leaflets appeared in the streets of Damascus during September 1994 calling for Syrians to prepare themselves for peace with Israel. "Peace is in the interests of the Republic of Syria and, among other things, it will lead to its economic development."[3] Significantly, the media, completely controlled by the regime, made no mention of these leaflets.

But Barry Rubin reads the tea leaves just the opposite, arguing that Syrian concessions to Israel "would undermine popular support" for the Assad regime.[4] Similarly, Fred Lawson sees domestic factors serving as "a brake" on Damascus accepting a U.S.-brokered agreement; he even interprets the regime's hard line in negotiations with Israel as a "way of buttressing its deteriorating domestic position."[5] Godfrey Jansen takes the matter a step further, characterizing Syrian feelings on the question of Israel as "perhaps the angriest in the Arab world, except for the [Palestinians in the] occupied territories."[6] Syrian leaders purport to find this latter interpretation more convincing. "We can only afford a just peace that is supported by the population," says Vice President 'Abd al-Halim Khaddam.' Syria's foreign minister, Faruq al-Sharaa, put it even more strongly: "the Syrian government wants peace more than its population."[8]

Syrian Policy

In all, with the notable exception of business interests, public sentiment appears to weigh against a decision for full and warm peace with Israel. The old dreams and fears remain too much alive to accept the Jewish state to a degree that begins to approach the Jordanian-Israeli peace or even the frigidity of the Egyptian-Israeli peace. The

---

[1] *International Herald Tribune*, October 11, 1994.

[2] *Reuter*, October 3, 1994.

[3] *Washington Times*, October 23, 1994.

[4] Barry Rubin, *Radical Middle East States and U.S. Policy*, Policy Paper Number Thirty-Five (Washington, DC: The Washington Institute for Near East Policy, 1993), 37.

[5] Fred H. Lawson, "Domestic Pressures and the Peace Process: Fillip or Hindrance?" in Eberhard Kienle, ed., *Contemporary Syria: Liberalization between Cold War and Cold Peace* (New York: St. Martin's Press, 1994), 140, 154.

[6] Godfrey Jansen, "Syria: Economic Revival, Political Stalemate," *Middle East International*, July 24, 1992, 15.

[7] *Der Spiegel*, July 10, 1995.

[8] Deborah Amos, *Lines in the Sand: Desert Storm and the Remaking of the Arab World* (New York: Simon and Schuster, 1992), 205.

Assad regime has the muscle to run roughshod over such sentiments, for, as Patrick Seale argues, Assad "is probably the only [Syrian leader] capable of turning around Syrian opinion and making his fellow-citizens accept the strategic decision for peace with the historic enemy."[1] But in offering Israel a cold peace without normalization Assad has so far shown no discernible intent to confront his population over this issue.

---

[1] Patrick Seale, "La Syrie et le processus de paix," *Politique Etrangère* (Winter 1992): 787.

APPENDIX IV

U.S. RELUCTANCE TO BLAME DAMASCUS FOR TERRORISM[1]

United States Department of State
INR/EC/RE
Washington, D.C. 20520
December 11, 1991

Mr. David Cohen
24 Elizabeth Street
Port Jervis, N.Y. 12771

Dear Mr. Cohen:

There is an official link between the Syrian Government and international terrorism which, to my knowledge, has never been publicly recognized.

During a Bureau of Intelligence and Research (INR) symposium for new analysts at Mr. Weather, Virginia during September 22-27, 1991, INR officers recounted their efforts to persuade Secretary of State James A. Baker III that the Syrian Government backed the terrorist group Dev Sol, the organization that murdered or wounded several Americans in Turkey during the war against Iraq.

Citing satellite photographs, INR prepared a series of reports for Secretary Baker's Morning Intelligence Summary in the Fall and Winter of 1990-1991. The pictures showed the face of a terrorist leader and a Dev Sol motto (in Turkish) drawn on the group of a military training camp in a region of Lebanon controlled by and just over the border from Syria. But Secretary Baker, they said, resisted the connection between Syria and Dev Sol, even when supported by other analysis. Finally, after unprecedented (and uncharacteristic) INR arm-twisting, Mr. Baker showed Hafez al-Assad, President of Syria, the pictures on a visit to the Middle East. Assad denied his Government's support for the Dev Sol training facility yet, shortly thereafter, new satellite imagery showed the face in the sand and the Dev Sol motto gone from the camp.

Although the foregoing is the sum of what I personnally know about the issue, you are welcome to contact me at home if you think I can help. My address is

4619 Yuma Street N.W.
Washington, D.C. 20016
Tel. (202) 686-4869

Sincerely yours,

J. Michael Springmann

---

[1] Letter from J. Michael Springmann to David Cohen, dated December 11, 1991.

<u>APPENDIX V</u>

U.S. SANCTIONS ON SYRIA

The U.S. government has applied many sanctions on Syria, some of them general regulations which apply to all states deemed to support terrorism or engaged in drug trafficking, others specifically aimed at Syria.[1]

General Sanctions Against States Supporting Terrorism

1. International Security Assistance and Arms Export Control Act of 1976: Section 303 terminates foreign assistance.

2. Export Administration Act of 1979: Section 6(i) requires the Executive Branch to notify Congress before licensing export of goods or technology valued at more than $7 million.

3. Omnibus Diplomatic Security and Antiterrorism Act of 1986: Section 509(a) prohibits military equipment sales.

4. Omnibus Budget Reconciliation Act of 1986: Section 8041(a) denies foreign tax credits on income or war profits.

5. Anti-Terrorism and Arms Export Control Amendments Act of 1989: Section 4 amends #2 above to require congressional notification for export of goods or technology of any value should such exports enhance military or terrorism capabilities.

6. Foreign Operations, Export Financing, and Related Programs Appropriations Act, 1995: Section 529 bans bilateral aid.

General Sanctions Against States Supporting Drug Trafficking

7. Anti-Drug Abuse Act of 1986: requires the president to draw up a list of states which have not cooperated in controlling drug production or trafficking, then prohibits aid and imposes trade restrictions on them along the same lines as those concerned with states supporting terrorism.

Sanctions Specific to Syria

8. Foreign Operations, Export Financing, and Related Programs Appropriations Act, 1995 (the latest in a series of foreign assistance appropriation acts since 1981 to bar Syria by name from receiving U.S. aid):

> Section 507 bars funds appropriated under this act from directly assisting eight countries, including Syria.

---

[1] This appendix simplifies the information found in Alfred B. Prados, "Syrian-U.S. Relations," Congressional Research Service Issue Brief No. 92075 updated to October 7, 1994.

Section 523 bars indirect assistance to nine countries, including Syria; it also permits a presidential waiver on national interest grounds, and this has in fact several times been exercised.

Section 528 directs U.S. representatives to vote against aid to such countries by international financial institutions (and does not allow for a presidential waiver).

9. Foreign Assistance Act of 1961, as amended by Section 431 of the Foreign Relations Authorization Act for FY 1994-1995: requires a withholding of contributions to international organizations for eight countries, including Syria.

As a result of these sanctions, the Department of Commerce lists thirty-three categories of exports that require validated license for shipping to Syria, including aircraft, vessels, most vehicles, parts, machine tools, computer equipment, and other high technology goods.

<u>APPENDIX VI</u>

SYRIAN SECURITY FORCES[1]

"Civilian" Agencies
- Bureau of National Security (*Maktab al-Amn al-Qawmi*) of the Ba'th Party, under Dr. 'Abd al-Ra'uf al-Kasm, prime minister until 1988 and the only Sunni to head an intelligence agency.
- General Intelligence Directorate (*Idarat al-Mukhabarat al-'Amma*), under Brig. Gen. Majid Sa'id until September 1994, now Maj. Gen. Bashir al-Najjar—probably the second most important agency.
- Political Security Directorate (*Idarat al-Amn al-Siyasi*), under Brig. Gen. 'Adnan Badr Hasan—probably the third most important agency.

Military Agencies
- Air Force Intelligence Directorate (*Idarat Mukhabarat al-Quwwa al-Jawiya*), under Brig. Gen. Muhammad al-Khuli until 1987, now under his nephew, Col. Ibrahim Huwaji.
- Military Intelligence (*Shu'bat al-Mukhabarat al-'Askariya*), under Brig. Gen. 'Ali Duba—probably the most important agency.
- Military Police (*al-Shurta al-'Askariya*), under Gen. Sari Rustum.
- Military Security (*al-Amn al-'Askariya*), under the command of the General Staff.

Military Units with Security Duties
- Defense Brigades of the Revolution (*Saraya al-Difa' 'an al-Thawra*), under Rif'at al-Assad, the president's brother until 1983, then under Mu'in Nassif, now disbanded.
- Republican Guard (*al-Haras al-Jumhuri*, sometimes called the Presidential Guard), the elite, division-size unit that protects the regime, under Assad's wife's brother, 'Adnan Makhluf.
- Special Forces (*al-Wahdat al-Khassa*), under Brig. Gen. 'Ali Haydar (an Alawi from Assad's home town of Qardaha) until July 1994, now under Maj. Gen, 'Ali Habib.
- Third Division (*al-Firqa al-Thalitha*), under Shafiq Fayyadh.

---

[1] This list derives from a chart in the *Middle East Quarterly* (September 1995): 59.

Policy Focus 15:   *Israel and the Gulf Crisis: Changing Security Requirements on the Eastern Front* by Dore Gold

Policy Focus 14:   *Iraq's Economic and Military Vulnerabilities* by Patrick Clawson and Seth Carus

Policy Focus 13:   *The Arab-Israeli Peace Process: A Trip Report* by Harvey Sicherman, Graeme Bannerman, Martin Indyk and Samuel Lewis

Policy Focus 12:   *Inside the PLO: Officials, Notables and Revolutionaries* by Barry Rubin

RECENT PUBLICATIONS OF THE WASHINGTON INSTITUTE

Making Peace with the PLO: The Rabin Government's Road to the Oslo Accord—An in-depth assessment of the personal, domestic, and international factors that led Yitzhak Rabin, Shimon Peres, and Israel's Labor government to conduct the secret negotiations that resulted in the historic Israeli-Palestinian peace accords, by *Jerusalem Post* diplomatic correspondent David Makovsky.

Intelligence and the Middle East: What Do We Need To Know?—A look at the changing needs and missions of the U.S. intelligence community in the post-Cold War Middle East. Includes presentations by Ellen Laipson, Daniel Kurtzer, and John L. Moore.

Supporting Peace: America's Role in an Israel-Syria Peace Agreement—A report on the role that U.S. forces could play in monitoring an Israel-Syria peace agreement by Michael Eisenstadt, Andrew Bacevich, and Carl Ford.

Approaching Peace: American Interests in Israeli-Palestinian Final Status Talks—A collection of essays presenting specific policy recommendations for Washington's role in reaching a final peace agreement. Contributors are Samuel Lewis, Hermann Eilts, Richard Haass, Peter Rodman, Eugene Rostow, William Quandt, Harvey Sicherman, and Kenneth Stein.

The Politics of Change in the Middle East—A collection of essays by distinguished scholars examining political stability and regime succession, edited by Robert Satloff.

For a complete list or to order publications, write or call:
The Washington Institute for Near East Policy
1828 L Street, NW, Suite 1050
Washington, D.C. 20036
Phone (202) 452-0650 ◊ Fax (202) 223-5364